ALLSTON-BRIGHTON
in
TRANSITION

ALLSTON-BRIGHTON
in
TRANSITION

From Cattle Town to Streetcar Suburb

Dr. William P. Marchione

Charleston   London

History
PRESS

Published by The History Press
Charleston, SC 29403
www.historypress.net

Cover image: *The Apostle's Oak* (1844). Oil painting by George Harvey. *Courtesy of the New York Historical Society*.

First published 2007

Manufactured in the United Kingdom

ISBN 978.1.59629.252.9

Library of Congress Cataloging-in-Publication Data

Marchione, William P., 1942-
  Allston-Brighton in transition : from cattle town to streetcar suburb
/
William P. Marchione.
     p. cm.
  ISBN 978-1-59629-252-9 (alk. paper)
  1. Allston (Boston, Mass.)--History--Anecdotes. 2. Brighton (Boston, Mass.)--History--Anecdotes. 3. Allston (Boston, Mass.)--Biography--Anecdotes. 4. Brighton (Boston, Mass.)--Biography--Anecdotes. 5. Allston (Boston, Mass.)--Buildings, structures, etc.--Anecdotes. 6. Brighton (Boston, Mass.)--Buildings, structures, etc.--Anecdotes. 7. Boston (Mass.)--History--Anecdotes. 8. Boston (Mass.)--Biography--Anecdotes. 9. Boston (Mass.)--Buildings, structures, etc.--Anecdotes. I. Title.
  F73.68.A44M36 2007
  974.4'61--dc22
                              2007003570

Notice: The information in this book is true and complete to the best of our knowledge. It is offered without guarantee on the part of the author or The History Press. The author and The History Press disclaim all liability in connection with the use of this book.

CONTENTS

Contents

PREFACE

It seems particularly appropriate to bring out this collection of Allston-Brighton historical articles in the year 2007, when the community is celebrating the two hundredth anniversary of its 1807 incorporation as the Town of Brighton.

Allston-Brighton has had a fascinating and, in many respects, unique history—a history so varied, so filled with twists and turns as to constitute a microcosm of our national experience. What Nathaniel Hawthorne noted of the Brighton Cattle Market in 1840—"It ought to be studied"—applies equally to the history of the community as a whole.

The thirty-two articles collected here under the title *Allston-Brighton in Transition: From Cattle Town to Streetcar Suburb* first appeared in the local press, most of them in the period 1998 to 2002, when I was writing regular bi-weekly columns for the *Allston-Brighton* and *Boston Tab* newspapers.

In organizing these articles, I tried to balance chronological and thematic considerations to provide a reasonably coherent account of Allston-Brighton's development, paralleling and elaborating on many of the themes I raised in my previous books on Allston-Brighton, while also introducing some new elements into the mix.

Readers will note that I sometimes invert the name Allston-Brighton to Brighton-Allston in these pages. This requires some explanation. I do this because the community's name has experienced many changes. From 1632 to 1807, we were part of Cambridge, called simply "Little Cambridge." In 1807, after 175 years of association with the parent community, we broke away to become the independent town of Brighton.

The separation was caused by the failure of Cambridge's town fathers to provide Little Cambridge with the network of roadways and bridges that it needed to protect the interests of its all-important cattle industry. The importance of the cattle trade to the history of the town in the nineteenth century cannot be overstated. This was the engine of the local economy and the town's cattle dealers and slaughterhouse proprietors were dominant figures. The name Brighton, one theory holds, references a variety of livestock, a "bright" or a prize ox.

The community bore the name Brighton from 1807 until 1867, when the name "Allston" was selected as a postal address for the eastern part of the community, the name being applied at about the same time to the local railroad depot. Residents now began referring to the eastern part of Brighton as Allston. It should be emphasized, however, that Allston never had a separate existence or even specific boundaries. There has accordingly been much confusion over the years about where Allston ends and Brighton begins.

Some time after Brighton's 1874 annexation by the City of Boston, city officials began the practice of referring to the city's new western district as "Allston-Brighton," thereby subordinating the name Brighton to a secondary position. The placing of the name Allston ahead of the name Brighton by city officials was no doubt occasioned by the geographical relationship of the city to its new western district—looking west from the metropolis, of course, Allston comes first, Brighton follows.

I dealt with this thorny nomenclature problem in these pages by referring to the community that we today call Allston-Brighton as "Little Cambridge" in the pre-1807 period, "Brighton" in the 1807 to 1874 period, "Brighton-Allston" down to about 1900 and as "Allston-Brighton" thereafter.

In closing, I would like to express my deepest appreciation to the board and membership of the Brighton-Allston Historical Society for the support and interest they have given my work as a local historian over the past thirty years, with special thanks to my wife, Mary Ann, herself an active and longstanding member of the BAHS Board, and to our children, David and Karen, for being so understanding and supportive of my three-decade-long obsession with local history.

1

JOHN ELIOT AND NONANTUM

Between 1646 and 1674, the Reverend John Eliot of Roxbury, the so-called Apostle to the Indians, converted some eleven hundred Massachusetts natives to the Christian religion and played a central role in establishing fourteen "Praying Indian" communities in the eastern part of Massachusetts.

Though not the first English missionary to attempt the conversion of New England's natives (that distinction belongs to Roger Williams of Rhode Island and Thomas Mayhew of Martha's Vineyard), the Roxbury clergyman had far more success than earlier missionaries, thanks largely to his unrivaled command of the native language, Algonquian.

Nor was Eliot content merely to preach to the natives in their own tongue. A fundamental tenet of the Puritan faith held that anyone seeking to know the will of God had to be able to read and interpret the Bible for himself. The natives had no written language into which Holy Scripture could be translated. Eliot dealt with this problem first by devising an Algonquian grammar (thus giving the language written form), and then by translating both the Old and New Testaments into that complex tongue, a herculean task that he did not finally complete until 1663.

There was also a measure of cultural imperialism in Eliot's approach to conversion, for the Roxbury minister required his converts to adopt an English style of living—to give up their semi-migratory habits and to settle into English-style villages under the watchful eye and rigid regulations of a Puritan church community.

The Reverend John Eliot, the Apostle to the Indians, is depicted here preaching to the natives of eastern Massachusetts. Eliot's first solid success as a missionary came in 1646 when he converted a band of local natives under Waban to Christianity and established his first Praying Indian community, Nonantum, on the present Brighton-Newton boundary. *Courtesy of the Brighton-Allston Historical Society Archives.*

Eliot also hoped to furnish each of these Praying Indian towns with a native minister. To that end, he helped found the Indian College at Harvard, an institution established specifically to train natives to preside over their own congregations. Another goal was the provision of schools in all the towns to ensure that the residents would be able to read the Bible for themselves.

John Eliot was born in Widford, Hertfordshire, England, in 1604, the younger son of Bennett Eliot, a wealthy landowner. When he was fifteen, he entered Jesus College at Cambridge University, where he quickly established a reputation as a brilliant linguist and classical scholar.

The early 1630s were a time of trouble for nonconformists, and in 1631 Eliot joined a great migration of Puritans to North America. Settling at first in Boston, he was immediately hired as a substitute for the Reverend John Wilson, who was then absent in England. When Wilson returned, the Boston congregation invited Eliot to remain in the capacity of an associate minister, but he instead opted to become the pastor of the church of neighboring Roxbury, a post he would occupy for nearly sixty years. Eliot also married at this point, his long and happy union with Ann (Mumford) Eliot lasting until his death in 1690 and producing six children.

John Eliot and Nonantum

The Roxbury minister's crusade to convert the local Indians was not launched until 1646, some fifteen years after his arrival in America, and one historian has suggested that Eliot's motives for delaying were as much political as religious.

In chartering the Bay Colony in 1628, the English government had extracted a solemn promise that conversion of the natives would be a high priority of the colonial regime (the seal of the Massachusetts Bay Colony, in fact, featured an Indian pleading with the English to "Come over and help us!"), but very little had been accomplished in the decade and a half after the colony's foundation.

The Bay Colony's leaders feared that the home government (which had fallen under the control of Presbyterian dictator Oliver Cromwell) might cancel some of Massachusetts's charter privileges unless a missionary crusade was soon launched. It was in this context that Eliot began to prepare himself for the task through a close study of the Algonquian language.

By 1646 Eliot was ready. His first attempt at conversion came in mid-1646, when he preached to a native community at Neponset in Dorchester under Sachem Cutshamekin, but this effort ended in embarrassing failure. Not only did the elderly Sachem reject Eliot's pleas to embrace Christianity, but his braves also openly ridiculed and heckled the clergyman.

At this point Eliot turned to another native leader, of somewhat lesser stature. At the urging of the Bay Colony magistrates, Eliot decided to proselytize Waban, son-in-law of the Sachem of Concord, whom he described as "one who gives more grounded hope of serious respect for the things of God, than any as yet I have known of that forlorn generation."

A small band under Waban lived on the southwest slope of Nonantum Hill (on the present Brighton-Newton boundary), an area that then formed part of Cambridge. It was in order to be closer to the white settlements that Waban's extended family had moved from his native Concord to the south side of the Charles River near Cambridge in the early 1630s.

Accompanying Eliot to Waban's encampment were three companions: Thomas Shepard, minister of Cambridge; Daniel Gookin, later supervisor of Indian towns for the Massachusetts Bay Colony; and either John Wilson, minister of Boston, or Elder Heath of Roxbury (on this point the record is unclear). The presence of these notables demonstrated the support that Eliot's missionary effort enjoyed from the Massachusetts Bay magistrates.

The date was October 18, 1646. A historic sermon initiated the Apostle's long crusade for the souls of the Massachusetts Bay natives. The three-hour lectureship—much of it delivered in the Algonquian tongue—had the anticipated effect. As his guests were leaving, recounted Reverend Shepard, Waban approached and said, "We need more ground to build our town on." To this Eliot responded, "I will speak to the General Court about that."

On November 4, 1646, the General Court of the Massachusetts Bay Colony voted to grant the desired land "for the good of the Indians" and appointed a commission, which included the Roxbury minister, to attend to the matter. When the Indians inquired what name to give their Christian village, Eliot recommended that it be called Nonantum, the Algonquian term for rejoicing, because the natives "hearing the word, and seeking to know God, the English did rejoice at it."

An early historian of Newton, the Reverend Jonathan Homer, has left us the following description of the Praying Indian village of Nonantum:

> *Mr. Eliot...furnished them, by the public aid, with shovels, spades, mattocks, and iron crows, and stimulated the most industrious with money...The houses of the meanest were found to be equal to those of the sachems or chiefs in other places. They surrounded the town with ditches...and with a stone-wall.*
>
> *The Indians, thus settled, were instructed in husbandry, and were excited to a prudent as well as industrious management of their affairs. Some of them were taught such trades as were most necessary for them, so that they completely built a house for public worship, 50 feet in length and 25 feet in breadth.*

Most of the financial support for Nonantum and for Eliot's other Praying Indian ventures came from the Society for the Propagation of the Gospel, based in England. The New England Puritans were much less sanguine of the long-range prospects for Christianizing the natives. Because of their deep distrust of the natives and the insatiable land hunger that marked the early history of the colony, the Praying Indian village of Nonantum soon proved untenable. In 1651, less than five years after its foundation, Eliot was obliged to move the entire population of this first Christian Indian community in British North America some fifteen miles to the southwest, to a three-thousand-acre site in the present-day town of Natick.

For the next quarter-century, the number of Eliot's Christian Indian communities proliferated until there were a total of fourteen. The Roxbury clergyman kept close watch over the progress of these settlements. The Praying Indian experiment was decisively undermined, however, by King Philip's War of 1675–76, the most severe Indian conflict in Massachusetts history, which led to the abandonment of most of Eliot's Praying Indian communities.

2

BRIGHTON'S REMARKABLE WINSHIPS

Brighton's Winship Street and Winship School commemorate the important contributions that four generations of Winships made to the community's history. Nineteenth-century Brighton was both the headquarters of New England's cattle trade and an important horticultural center, and the Winships were responsible for founding both of these local industries.

Less well known, but of perhaps even broader historical significance, were the contributions the Winships made to the Pacific trade. For a time the members of this Brighton family were so dominant in that trade that they were referred to as the Lords of the Pacific.

The Winships, who hailed originally from Lexington, settled in Brighton (then called Little Cambridge) just before the outbreak of the American Revolution. Cambridge, of course, served as the headquarters of the Continental army from 1775 to 1776, and General Washington's troops badly needed provisions. Jonathan Winship I and Jonathan Winship II, father and son, responded by putting out a call to the farmers of Middlesex County, as well as other outlying areas, to send their cattle to Little Cambridge. As this livestock arrived, the Winships purchased and processed it for the army.

The importance of the Winship contribution to the Patriot cause was noted by Willard M. Wallace in his military history of the Revolution: "There were so few hungry soldiers in the siege lines around Boston that winter that one might say it was with food rather than with troops and arms that Washington kept the British locked up in the city."

The Winship Mansion, seen here, was situated on the site of the present District 14 Police Station, just east of Brighton Center, and was the focal point of a thriving hundred-acre farmstead. It was built in 1780 by Jonathan Winship I and Jonathan Winship II, father and son, the founders of the Brighton Cattle Market. *Courtesy of the Brighton-Allston Historical Society Archives.*

The Little Cambridge Cattle Market continued to prosper after the war. By 1790 Jonathan Winship II had become the largest meatpacker in Massachusetts, putting up some five thousand barrels of beef a year for foreign markets alone.

It was the next generation of Winships that ventured into the Pacific. From 1796 to 1816, Jonathan Winship II's four sons—Abiel, Charles, Nathan and Jonathan III—outfitted and directed a succession of daring Pacific expeditions, ventures so energetic that maritime historian Samuel Eliot Morison was prompted to label these men "the remarkable Winship brothers."

Abiel (1769–1824), the eldest of the four, initiated these expeditions through his Boston-based mercantile house, Homer and Winship. As early as 1795, when "Trader Abiel" was still in his twenties, he held a major interest in eight vessels engaged in trade with Europe and the West Indies. Although Abiel never ventured into the Pacific himself, his keen business sense paved the way for his younger brothers who had a significant impact on the Pacific trade.

These adventures began in 1799, when Charles Winship set sail for the Pacific as supercargo of an 111-ton brig, *Betsey*, owned by Homer and Winship, reputedly the first American vessel to unfurl the U.S. flag upon the upper and lower California coasts.

The Winships were lured to Spanish California by the prospects of huge profits from seal and otter hunting. A ready market for the sleek pelts of these animals existed in China. While this initial voyage proved profitable, it also ended in personal tragedy for the Winships when Charles, jailed by the *Guarda Costal* for poaching in Spanish coastal waters, contracted "a malignant fever of the climate" and died at the age of twenty-three. The Winships were put off by this tragedy not one wit, however.

A problem that needed to be resolved if the future profits of this trade were to be maximized was the relative lack of skill that American crewmembers possessed when it came to hunting, slaughtering and skinning seals and otters.

This difficulty was overcome through collaboration with Alexander Baranov, the governor of Russian America (Alaska). An arrangement was worked out with the Russian official whereby he would furnish the Winships with Aleut hunters for seal hunting and skinning, in exchange for badly needed supplies and firearms.

The Russian colony was in dire condition in the early 1800s. It had not been provisioned from its home base in several years and was facing severe shortages. In addition, its various settlements were threatened by hostile natives. Joseph O'Cain, an Anglo-Irish mariner familiar with the situation, brought it to the attention of the Winships. Abiel not only eagerly embraced the idea of opening up trade with Russian America, but also undertook to outfit a 280-ton vessel specifically for that purpose, naming it the *O'Cain*, after the man who was to serve as its first captain. Jonathan Winship III (1780–1847) was sent along as first mate on this initial expedition.

For the next six years the Winships engaged in this highly profitable trade with Alaska. Jonathan III captained the *O'Cain* in all but the first of these voyages. The provisions and firearms the Winships carried to Russian America have been credited with saving that colony from extinction.

The most profitable of the various Winship Pacific expeditions was that of 1805–08. When the *O'Cain* arrived at Canton, China, in December 1807, it carried a cargo of pelts valued at more than $136,000, an enormous sum for that day. This voyage marked the apogee of the family's fortunes in the Pacific trade. After 1808, the position of the Winships in the Pacific steadily deteriorated in the face of formidable competition and a series of misfortunes.

For one thing, the Winships had hoped to secure a monopoly in the trade with Russian-America, but Governor Baranov proved firmly resistant to the idea. (The Russian imperial government did not wish the colony to become permanently dependent upon Yankee traders.) Moreover, by 1808 the general situation was changing. The number of vessels in the Pacific (both American and foreign) was on the rise, creating a much more competitive situation.

A portrait of Captain Jonathan Winship, dating from 1850, by Thomas Badger. One of the "Remarkable Winship Brothers," after returning from the Pacific after the War of 1812, Jonathan III formed a partnership with his younger brother Francis and founded Winships' Gardens, Brighton's pioneer horticultural establishment, a facility described as an early version of the Arnold Arboretum. *Courtesy of the Brighton-Allston Historical Society Archives.*

The Winships, however, were not about to give up. They sought to offset these disadvantages by establishing a trading station at a midpoint on the northwest coastline, a station that would be both close at hand and well-supplied with Yankee goods, thereby giving them a competitive edge in dealing with the Russians. The location they selected was the Columbia River Valley.

In 1809 a second Winship vessel, the *Albatross*, was dispatched to the Pacific under the command of Nathan Winship (1778–1820) with instructions to build and provision a fort and trading post on the Columbia. Construction of the facility was begun in May 1810, at a point some forty miles up the river, opposite present-day Oak Point, Washington.

This imaginative plan was doomed, however, by unforeseen developments. First, only four days after construction began, floodwaters inundated the site. Then, when work was resumed on higher ground, a mass of hostile Chinook warriors (who feared their displacement as middlemen in the local fur trade) prompted Captain Nathan to abandon the building project altogether.

Had the Winships succeeded in establishing this trading post on the Columbia, it would have been the first permanent settlement by white men on that river, predating John Jacob Astor's Fort Astoria by several months.

After leaving the Columbia, the *Albatross* traded along the northwest coast until October 1811, when it crossed to Honolulu. Here it rendezvoused with the *O'Cain* and a third Winship vessel, the *Isabella*. The flotilla then added Hawaiian sandalwood to its cargoes. A ready market for sandalwood existed in China, where it was used in incense burners as part of Chinese religious rituals.

The Winships had earlier assisted the king of the Hawaiian Islands, Kamehameha I, in his negotiations with local rulers to secure the unification of the island chain. In July 1812, Kamehameha granted the Winships, whom he trusted and liked, the exclusive right to export sandalwood from Hawaii. However, with the outbreak of the War of 1812, the British, who enjoyed naval dominance in the Pacific, pressured the Hawaiian monarch into canceling this potentially lucrative monopoly.

The War of 1812 administered the coup de grâce to the declining fortunes of the Winships. After 1813, their vessels were effectively driven off the high seas by the powerful British fleet. The *O'Cain*, under Captain Jonathan Winship, eventually took refuge in Whampoa (Canton), China. It was here that Jonathan, during a period of forced leisure, acquired the skills in horticulture that led to his founding in 1820, in partnership with his youngest brother Francis, of Winships' Gardens, Brighton's pioneer horticultural enterprise. Later, Captain Jonathan Winship also played a key role in the founding of the Massachusetts Horticultural Society, serving as that organization's vice-president from 1835 until his death in 1847.

3

WHEN CATTLE WAS KING

One of New England's great institutions, the Brighton Cattle Market, was founded in mid-1776, when a father-and-son team, Jonathan Winship I and Jonathan Winship II, put out a call to the farmers of Middlesex County urging them to slaughter their cattle and send the resulting meat supply to the village of Little Cambridge (later renamed Brighton) to help feed General George Washington's soldiers. The British had just evacuated Boston, and the Army of New England, then headquartered in and around the liberated city, was in desperate need of provisions of all kinds.

Why was Little Cambridge selected as the point of delivery for this meat supply? The village, then still a part of Cambridge, lay just outside of Boston, astride the main road (the Watertown Highway, now called Washington Street), linking the metropolis to its western hinterland. It was therefore a logical collection point.

The enterprising Winships, who held a contract from the U.S. government to supply meat for the army, soon realized, however, that there was more money to be made from doing the slaughtering themselves, which, of course, necessitated the establishment of a local slaughterhouse. The cattle and slaughtering trades, which the Winships launched in 1776, quickly transformed the sleepy agricultural village of Little Cambridge into a thriving commercial center. The selling and butchering of cattle became the economic mainstay of the town for more than a century, profoundly influencing virtually every aspect of Brighton's economic, political and social development.

The first stockyard in Brighton was laid out next to the Bull's Head Tavern, an inn that stood on the site of 201 Washington Street, about a quarter of a mile east of Brighton Center.

The cattle pens probably stood on the flat land opposite the tavern (Nantasket Avenue, Snow and Shannon Streets cross the acreage today), where a stream provided a convenient water supply for the livestock.

The Winship slaughterhouse stood at the foot of nearby Powder House Hill (now called Academy Hill), at the southeast corner of present-day Chestnut Hill Avenue and Academy Hill Road.

In her reminiscences of Brighton in the late 1820s, Mary Jane Kingsley Merwin provides the only description of the Winship Slaughterhouse known to exist. The oldest slaughterhouse in Brighton was by then long abandoned. "Open the gate [to Powder House Hill]. On your left is the old slaughterhouse fast falling to decay. The floors have mostly gone, the timbers are rotting and the doors have mostly fallen from the rusty hinges. The grounds all around are covered with Mayweed."

The Winship family stockyard and slaughtering enterprises were immediately successful. As early as 1777, as the records of the Army of New England indicate, the family's two warehouses in Little Cambridge contained some five hundred barrels of salted beef. So important was this

Brighton Center in 1832. The building to the left is the Cattle Fair Hotel, as it looked before its 1850 enlargement. At the center of this engraving stands the First Parish Church, constructed in 1808. At the extreme right one sees the Bank of Brighton, the town's first bank, which handled the cattle trade transactions that were such an important feature of Brighton's nineteenth-century economy. *Courtesy of the Brighton-Allston Historical Society Archives.*

meat supply to the Revolutionary cause that the army posted soldiers in Little Cambridge to protect it against possible sabotage.

In 1780 Jonathan Winship II built an elaborate residence at the eastern end of the village (on the site of the present District 14 Police Station), a short distance from the stockyard. "This Winship Mansion," one source notes, "was in its day a house of much importance, and was surrounded by a large tract of highly cultivated land; besides, rich, well-stocked pastures, on which browsed many varieties of fancy cattle." The Winship estate comprised more than one hundred acres.

By 1790 Jonathan II (the elder Jonathan had died in 1784) was the largest meatpacker in Massachusetts, putting up some five thousand barrels of beef a year for foreign markets alone.

Other slaughterhouses soon made their appearance. By the 1860s, there were more than forty such establishments scattered over the town.

The success of the cattle and slaughtering trades was reinforced by three major events of the early nineteenth century: Brighton's separation from Cambridge on February 24, 1807, placing local government firmly in the hands of the town's cattle and slaughtering interests; the selection of Brighton in 1818 as the permanent headquarters of the fairgrounds and exhibition hall of the Massachusetts Society for Promoting Agriculture, site of the annual Brighton Fair and Cattle Show, the state's most important agricultural gathering; and the construction through the town in 1834 of the Boston and Worcester Railroad, which soon after began carrying livestock to its Brighton Depot.

Herds of livestock converged on Brighton from every direction: Rhode Island, Cape Cod, New Hampshire, Vermont, Maine, even eastern Canada, often to the consternation of the residents of nearby towns.

By the 1820s, the Brighton Cattle Market was receiving two thousand to eight thousand head of cattle every week. Monday was Market Day, and the traffic on the roads to Brighton reached such proportions that the clergymen of the country towns complained of Sabbath day noise and confusion, when "the lowing of herds, the bleating of flocks, the redounding lash, and the drover's voice and whistle, discordantly mingle with the songs of the temple."

In 1828 the *New England Farmer* estimated the value of cattle sold at Brighton, principally for slaughter, over less than two months at $540,000, an enormous sum at the time. Another source tells us that the average sale of cattle at the Brighton Cattle Market from 1835 to 1845 exceeded $2 million a year.

Brighton was the chief market for livestock in New England, and it was a common sight to see herds of cattle, sheep and other varieties of livestock driven through Brookline Village and up Washington Street to Brighton. Starting down in Rhode Island with a few head, cattle were picked up from farmers along the road so that the herd was at its maximum through Brookline.

About 1820, the stockyard was moved from its original location at the Bull's Head Tavern to the rear of the Hastings Tavern on the north side of Washington Street in Brighton Center, just east of present-day Leicester Street. In 1830 the old tavern was replaced by the Cattle Fair Hotel, managed by Zachariah B. Porter, who later operated Cambridge's Porter House Hotel, the man for whom Porter Square and the porterhouse steak were named.

In 1852 the Cattle Fair Hotel was magnificently enlarged in the Italianate style by noted Boston architect William Washburn. Its one hundred rooms made it the largest hostelry in the Boston suburbs—the most opulent by far of a score of Brighton hotels established to accommodate the patrons of the town's burgeoning cattle and slaughtering trades.

To the rear of the Cattle Fair Hotel were ten acres of livestock pens and barns. Here Brighton's town auctioneer, standing atop a raised platform, officiated every market day as thousands of head of livestock were sold to the highest bidder.

4

NATHANIEL HAWTHORNE VISITS THE BRIGHTON CATTLE MARKET

The most engaging and insightful contemporary descriptions of the colorful Brighton Cattle Market came from the pen of one of New England's greatest writers, Nathaniel Hawthorne, who visited the market on two occasions in the early 1840s. These accounts first appeared in Hawthorne's *American Note-Book.*

The writer's first visit occurred in October 1840. He may well have stayed at the Cattle Fair Hotel on this first visit. The 1840 account is also the more polished of the two, and is the one most frequently quoted:

> *Thursday of every week which by common consent and custom is market day changes the generally quiet village of Brighton into a scene of bustle and excitement. At early morning the cattle, sheep, etc. are hurried in and soon the morning train from Boston, omnibuses, carriages, and other "vehicular mediums" bring a throng of drovers, buyers, speculators and spectators; so that by 10 o'clock, there are generally gathered as many as two or three hundred vehicles in the area fronting the Cattle Fair Hotel.*

The denizens of the Brighton Cattle Market were heavy drinkers, wrote Hawthorne, and the Cattle Fair Hotel bar very much a focal point of market-day activities. "The proprietors [of the hotel] throng the spacious barroom for the purpose of warming themselves in winter, and in summer 'cooling off'—the process for effecting both results being precisely the same."

The hotel portico and adjacent area, Hawthorne tells us, accommodated an early version of a flea market, with hawkers and peddlers selling a variety of wares at bargain prices—clothing, jewelry, soap, watches, knives, razors and the like. Another feature was an exhibit of unusual and bizarre items such as a "Mammoth Steer," a "Living Skeleton," a display of reptiles, etc., all available "at reasonable prices."

Then there was the infamous Brighton horse auction. The buying and selling of horseflesh was an important business in the market town. "A Brighton horse had become a proverb," Hawthorne observed, with mildly disapproving amusement.

> *Here are gathered old, worn out, broken-down, and used up omnibus, cart, and livery stable steeds, and these are knocked down (if they don't tumble down) at sums varying from five to thirty dollars. These sales are productive of a great deal of merriment and the mettle, speed, and fine points of these animals are exhibited (the "points" perhaps being sufficiently prominent already).*

The heart of the cattle market—the stockyard area behind the hotel, with its raised auction platform—was caught up in a constant whirl of activity.

FORE SAIL.

"A Brighton horse has become a proverb," wrote Nathaniel Hawthorne in 1840. This illustration of a Brighton horse from a *Harper's Weekly* article of the following decade illustrates Hawthorne's point perfectly. *Courtesy of the Brighton-Allston Historical Society Archives.*

The fattest and best of the cattle in their pens find ready sale, and long before all the drovers are in, select lots begin to be driven from the grounds. Men and boys hurry up and down the lanes and through the pens, each armed with a stick which is a sort of shillelagh, shouting to the half-crazed cattle, and with screams and blows directing them where they should go. Occasionally a drove of cows and calves come along, the latter muzzled, and the former looing and bellowing in chorus to the shouts of the drivers.

At noon a bell was rung announcing dinner, which signaled a breathing spell for participants. After dinner, trading resumed, but the pace of activity began tapering off. "By five o'clock the business of the day is over," wrote Hawthorne, "and Brighton subsides once more into a quiet matter-of-fact Massachusetts village, till another Thursday brings round another market day."

At the time of the author's second, September 1841, visit, he was living at Brook Farm, the famous utopian community in West Roxbury. Market day in the meantime had been moved from Thursdays to Mondays out of concern for the town's schoolchildren. Brighton, in contrast to other towns, maintained a Tuesday through Saturday school schedule so as not to expose the town's students to the dangers associated with cattle drives.

Hawthorne and his traveling companion, William B. Allen, made the five-mile journey to Brighton early Monday morning by wagon, with the practical object of selling a calf and buying four piglets. "It was an ugly thought," the author noted dryly of the tiny calf he was carrying to Brighton, which he described as an "affectionate creature," that its "confidence in human nature was to be so ill-rewarded as by cutting its throat, and selling him in quarters."

What route did Hawthorne and his associate follow in traveling from West Roxbury to Brighton in 1841? An examination of old maps would suggest that they wound their way to the Brighton Cattle Market via Brookline's LaGrange and Hammond Streets, the old Worcester Turnpike (now Boylston Street or Route 9) and Chestnut Hill Avenue, which was then called Rockland Street. This early morning journey must have taken at least two hours, for on Mondays the road to Brighton was crowded "with cows, oxen, sheep, and pigs for Brighton Fair."

The author described the countryside that he and his companion traversed as both attractive and prosperous—an area of "warm and comfortable farmhouses...modern cottages, smart and tasteful; and villas with terraces before them and...wooden urns on pillars, and other such tokens of gentility."

Nathaniel Hawthorne Visits the Brighton Cattle Market

The great writer Nathaniel Hawthorne visited the Brighton Cattle Market twice in the early 1840s, writing the most detailed description of that famous New England institution. *Courtesy of the Brighton-Allston Historical Society Archives.*

On entering Brighton, Hawthorne found the village "thronged with people, horses, and vehicles." Nowhere in New England, he noted of the cattle center, was the true character of the agricultural population so clearly revealed.

> *Almost all the farmers, within a reasonable distance, make it a point, I suppose, to attend Brighton fair pretty frequently, if not on business, yet*

as amateurs. Then there are the cattle people and the butchers who supply the Boston Market, and the dealers from far and near, and every man who has a cow or a yoke of oxen, whether to sell or buy, goes to Brighton on Monday.

Hawthorne's 1841 description of the Brighton Cattle Market was more concerned with the human comedy of the scene than the details of the purchase and sale of livestock.

The yeomen seemed to be more in their element than I have ever seen them anywhere else. Most of the attendees were of a bulky make, with much bone and muscle, and some good store of fat. There were, in addition, gentlemen farmers, neatly, trimly, and fashionably dressed; yeomen in their black and blue country suits, cut by country tailors, and awkwardly worn; country loafers, who looked wistfully at the liquor in the bar, [waiting] for some friend to invite them to drink; also, dandies from the city, stayed and buckramed, who had come to see the humors of the Brighton Fair.

Hawthorne concluded this second description evidencing that he possessed a historian's sensibilities in abundance: "All the scene of this fair was very characteristic and peculiar—cheerfully and lively too, in the bright sun. I must see it again. It ought to be studied."

5

Hannah Foster
Brighton's Pioneer Novelist

Few local residents realize that number 10 Academy Hill Road, just outside of Brighton Center, is a major American literary landmark. Time has not been kind to this ancient edifice, which once served as the parsonage of Brighton's First Parish Church. Its western façade, facing Academy Hill Road, was long ago converted into a storefront.

What makes this building so important? Here in 1797, Hannah Webster Foster, the wife of Brighton's minister, the Reverend John Foster, wrote a pioneer American novel entitled *The Coquette, or the History of Eliza Wharton.*

Not only was *The Coquette* the first novel ever written by a native-born American woman, but its publication also caused a literary sensation.

The Coquette was a thinly veiled account (employing fictitious names) of the seduction, betrayal and eventual death in childbirth of Elizabeth Whitman, daughter of the Reverend Elnathon Whitman of Hartford, Connecticut (a distant relative of Reverend John Foster). Her seducer, it was generally believed, was Pierpont Edwards, son of the great evangelical minister Jonathan Edwards, the preacher who spearheaded the religious movement known as the Great Awakening. The reputation of Pierpont's father as a moral arbiter, of course, added spice to the Whitman scandal. Then, as now, scandal exerted a powerful attraction upon the reading public.

The Coquette was said to have been, next to the Bible, the most popular reading material of early nineteenth-century New England. A recent commentator tells us that it was "one of the two best-selling American novels of the 18th century." By 1840 it had appeared in some thirty editions!

Title page to the original edition of Hannah Webster Foster's 1797 novel *The Coquette, or The History of Eliza Wharton*, written at the First Church Parsonage, on Academy Road, Brighton. *Courtesy of the Brighton-Allston Historical Society Archives.*

But *The Coquette* was much more than a potboiler. The work also had genuine literary merit. As the editor of its 1970 edition, William Osborne, noted, "Mrs. Foster [gave] early American fiction an interest it did not have before: a candid discussion of a social problem and a sensible depiction of character." Cathy N. Davidson, professor of English at Michigan State College, in her introduction to the most recent (1986) edition of *The Coquette*, added that it realistically examined "the parameters of female powerlessness and female constraint" in late eighteenth-century American society.

Hannah Webster Foster was born in Salisbury, Massachusetts, in 1758, the daughter of Grant Webster, a well-to-do Boston merchant and moneylender, and Hannah Wainwright Webster. After her mother's death in 1762, Hannah was sent to a boarding school for several years, an experience that provided the basis of her second novel, also written at 10 Academy Hill Road, *The Boarding School, or, Lessons of a Preceptress to Her Pupils*, published in 1799.

The wealth of the Webster family was evidenced by an advertisement her father ran in the *Massachusetts Sun* in 1771, offering a wide assortment of goods and property for sale, including produce, ship supplies, several Boston tenements, a country estate ten miles outside of the city and a Suffolk County lead mine. Hannah's brother, Redford Webster, who made his own fortune in the drug business, resided in the Clarke-Frankland mansion in Boston's fashionable North Square. Only in the next generation did the Webster family fall upon hard times, when Redford's son, Dr. John Webster, was judged guilty of the bludgeoning death of Dr. John Parkman and was sentenced to be hanged in the most famous Boston murder trial of the nineteenth century.

Hannah Webster married Reverend John Foster of Little Cambridge in 1785, a year after the recent Dartmouth College graduate assumed the pulpit of that community's First Parish Church.

Reverend and Mrs. Foster occupied three Brighton residences during their forty-four-year marriage. Their first home was the old Ebenezer Smith House at 15–17 Peaceable Street, a structure that still stands, the oldest building in the Brighton Center area. Originally the home of major Brighton landowner Ebenezer Smith, this historic structure had accommodated the Winships from 1775 to 1780, at the time of their founding of the Brighton Cattle Market.

About 1790 the Fosters moved to the newly constructed and much larger First Church Parsonage at 10 Academy Hill Road, where Hannah was to write her two novels in the 1797 to 1799 period. With the publication of her second novel, however, Hannah's career as a writer came to an abrupt end. Her time thereafter was devoted to raising a large family and attending to the myriad responsibilities of a minister's wife.

Then, about 1810, John and Hannah built an elaborate mansion on Foster Street, originally called Seaver Lane, probably with money inherited from her father. This building stood on the site of the Franciscan Missionary Society for Africa convent, a location a contemporary described as "overlooking scenery as charming as in any part of Brighton." The Foster Mansion has been described as "a very large square house which faced to the south, to the front porch of which was added an ell used as a library and a reception room. The hilly land east of the house was terraced and the daughters became very industrious in keeping the grounds well stocked with flowering shrubs and plants." Another source noted that it was "just the place for a minister to write a sermon and romantic enough for a wife to write a novel." While the bulk of the Foster Mansion was taken down in 1848, to make way for another structure, a portion of the old house still stands across the road at 181 Foster Street.

Hannah and John Foster had six children, three sons and three daughters. Two of the daughters, Hannah Foster Cheney and Elizabeth Foster Cushing, followed in their mother's footsteps and became writers.

Prior to 1827, Reverend Foster presided over the only church in Brighton. As the wife of the town's only minister and the daughter of an important Boston merchant, Hannah became the acknowledged social leader of the community. Her role outside the household was largely confined to church-related activities.

In her reminiscences of the town in the 1820s, Mary Jane Kingsley Merwin underscored the social prominence the Fosters enjoyed by recounting the anxiety her parents, the Kingsleys, experienced at the prospect of a social call by the Fosters. The Kingsley household spent a week preparing for this signal social event. Some sources contend that the "aristocratic" Fosters had an exclusive attitude that served to offend many of the town's residents.

Whatever the case, it seems clear that Hannah Foster took her social responsibilities quite seriously. A history of the Massachusetts Federation of Women's Clubs credits her with having founded—in the early 1800s, among the female members of her husband's Brighton church—the first women's club in Massachusetts.

In 1827 a schism occurred in Brighton's First Parish Church, when a breakaway group established the Brighton Evangelical Congregational Society. A short time later Reverend Foster, who was in his sixties and in failing health, relinquished his pulpit. After his death in 1829, Hannah moved to Montreal to live with her daughter, Elizabeth Foster Cushing, the wife of Dr. Frederick Cushing, who was the physician at the Emigrant Hospital there. Hannah Webster Foster, Brighton's pioneer novelist, died in Montreal in 1840, at age eighty-one.

6

Oak Square's Daniel Bowen
Boston's Pioneer Museum Keeper

Contemporary Boston is a city of many great museums. The history of museum keeping in the Hub had its modest beginnings in 1791, with the arrival from Philadelphia of one Daniel Bowen, age thirty-one, a close friend of the patriot-painter Charles Willson Peale, the nation's pioneer museum keeper.

It has been suggested that Bowen left Philadelphia to avoid competing with his good friend. But whereas Peale's contributions to the field of museum keeping have been widely heralded by historians, those of Bowen have received scant attention.

The details of Bowen's early life are obscure. One source refers to him as "Daniel Bowen, sea fighter of the Revolution, who had been in and about [Philadelphia] with a waxworks show after the peace, intent upon making his fortune."

In addition to wax figures, Bowen brought to Boston several canvasses by the recently deceased English painter Robert Edge Pine (1730–1788), as well as ample financial resources, which he may have gained as a Revolutionary War privateer.

That he was financially well off is demonstrated by his purchase, shortly after his arrival, of a nine-acre estate, Lime Grove, in the part of Cambridge that in 1807 became the town of Brighton. This estate stood on the south side of Washington Street just above Oak Square. The mansion house stood at the point where Tip Top Street intersects Washington Street today. Since he apparently never owned a residence in the city proper, Bowen may be considered one of Boston's earliest suburban commuters.

Museum keeping was then a lot less specialized than it is today. The nation's earliest museums featured everything from paintings to waxen figures, to stuffed animals and birds, to public lectures and performances, to animal and variety acts—all manner of exotica mixed together for the edification and diversion of an entertainment-starved public.

Daniel Bowen's museum had its modest beginnings in an exhibit of wax figures and paintings that he mounted in 1791 at the American Coffee House, a popular tavern located on the north side of State Street, opposite the intersection of Kilby Street.

Above: Bowen's Brighton residence, called "Lime Grove," stood on Washington Street just west of Oak Square, where Tip Top Street now intersects Washington Street. *Courtesy of the SPNEA / Historic New England.*

Opposite: Daniel Bowen of Brighton, pioneer Boston museum keeper, who established the Columbian Museum in 1791. *Courtesy of the Brighton-Allston Historical Society Archives.*

The waxen figures displayed in this first exhibit included representations of George Washington, Benjamin Franklin and John Adams. That of local favorite Adams had "on either side of him Liberty with staff and cap and Justice with sword and balance." David and Goliath were the subjects of another waxen display, with the figure of Goliath standing some twelve feet high.

As more space became available, figures representing *The Sleeping Nymph* and *The Salem Beauty* as well as characters from popular literature were added to Bowen's waxworks. By the mid-1790s, with public outrage against Jacobin France at an all-time high, figures were added showing the condemned French King Louis XVI bidding farewell to his family, as well as that of a man being guillotined.

Space in the American Coffee House being limited, it was not long before Bowen moved his collection to more ample quarters in a hall on the top floor of a schoolhouse on nearby Hollis Street.

Museum keeping was a lucrative profession only if the public could be induced to make repeated visits. This meant a constant addition of new exhibits, which required additional space. Thus Bowen moved his establishment a third time, in 1795, to a "large and elegant hall" at the corner of Bromfield and Tremont Streets, opposite Paddock's Mall, fronting the Granary Burying Ground, a popular promenade of the day.

One of the principal attractions of the museum's new Tremont Street facility was a huge painting depicting *Columbia*, symbol of the republic, mourning the ravages of the war then being waged between Britain and France, a conflict highly damaging to oceangoing trade, which was the economic lifeblood of Boston. Mr. Bowen's Museum, as it was commonly called, was renamed the Columbian in 1801, possibly at the time of the dedication of this massive canvas.

However, there was much more to the Columbian Museum than waxen figures and a picture gallery. Public entertainments and lectures were also staged there, including occasional dramatic performances and variety acts.

One exhibit, more suggestive of P.T. Barnum than the sedate offerings of a modern museum, featured a bibulous elephant who consumed vast quantities of spirituous liquor, the museum's advertising assuring the public that "thirty bottles of porter, of which he draws the corks himself, is not an uncommon allowance." All of this, needless to say, occurred in the days before the establishment of the MSPCA!

Despite such vulgarities, Bowen's Museum is said to have had a significant influence on the history of American painting. The works of art on display there, especially those of Robert Edge Pine, formed the only public art gallery in Boston. Art historians credit this collection with influencing three major painters: Washington Allston, the great Romantic painter; Samuel F.B. Morse, better known as the inventor of the telegraph; and Edward Greene Malbone, a miniaturist of note, all of whom resided in the Boston area in the 1790s.

Another great artistic contribution that Daniel Bowen rendered Boston was in the inducement of his nephew, Abel Bowen, a highly talented wood engraver, to move to Brighton from New York in 1812. Abel's first workshop in Boston was established in the Columbian Museum, and several of his earliest works were created to advertise museum exhibits and performances. For the next almost forty years, Abel Bowen created a series of handsome wood engravings of Boston's principal landmarks that compose an important part of the city's historical legacy.

On January 15, 1803, the Columbian Museum's Tremont Street building was destroyed in a spectacular fire that also consumed the entire collection. This conflagration was so huge that its glow could be seen from Portsmouth, New Hampshire, seventy miles away. Daniel Bowen, however, demonstrated remarkable resilience in the face of this frightful disaster, for within five months his Columbian Museum was back in business on the second floor of a building on Milk Street, opposite the Old South Church.

This was but a temporary home, however. Wishing to reestablish his business on Tremont Street, near the mall, Bowen proceeded to build a five-story brick structure on a lot east of the King's Chapel Burying Ground. His partner in this venture was W.M.S. Doyle. This large structure, some 34 feet wide and 108 feet deep, rose to the commanding height of 84 feet. The top of the new Columbian Museum building featured an observatory, surmounted by a statue of Minerva, the Roman goddess of wisdom and crafts. Bowen dedicated the impressive new edifice with much fanfare on November 27, 1806.

On January 16, 1807, less than two months after its opening, Bowen's second Tremont Street headquarters suffered the same fate as its predecessor. The flames that consumed the 1806 building were said to have erupted from equipment set up for a show called *The Phantasmagoria*, involving "spectreology and dancing witches."

Even more tragic than the destruction of the museum and its contents, was the heavy loss of life this fire exacted. A large crowd of spectators had gathered in the King's Chapel Burying Ground to watch the show's progress, when one of the walls of the museum collapsed into their midst, burying nine boys between the ages of ten and fifteen. In true Puritan fashion, Boston voices cried out that such displays as *The Phantasmagoria* were sacrilegious and that a wrathful God had exacted a fitful punishment on Boston.

Here again, however, Daniel Bowen demonstrated incredible resilience, for by June 2, 1807, a new two-story Columbian Museum stood on the same site. Bowen operated this more modest facility in partnership with Doyle until 1815, at which point, for reasons not entirely clear, he sold his share of the museum, disposed of his Brighton estate and left Boston permanently. Bowen was fifty-five years of age when he departed Boston. The museum survived under Doyle's management for another ten years, at which point it was bought by its rival, the New England Museum.

As to Daniel Bowen, Boston's pioneer museum keeper, he lived on to the ripe old age of ninety-six, dying in Philadelphia in 1856.

7

BRIGHTON'S AGRICULTURAL HALL
A Farming Landmark

At the southeast corner of Washington Street and Chestnut Hill Avenue in Brighton Center stands one of Brighton's oldest and most historic buildings. Originally known as Agricultural Hall, this 1818 edifice now houses a variety of shops and businesses.

A few years ago, the building's current owner, Steve Wasserman, completed a major and highly sensitive renovation of the landmark structure, giving it an appearance more appropriate to its original Greek Revival design.

When Agricultural Hall was built in the second decade of the nineteenth century, the town of Brighton was an important farming and cattle marketing center, a major producer of vegetables, fruit and meat for Boston's burgeoning population.

Two years before the construction of Agricultural Hall, the Massachusetts Society for Promoting Agriculture (MSPA)—the state's oldest agricultural organization—chose Brighton as the site for its annual fair and cattle show. One of the earliest and largest agricultural fairs in the nation, the MSPA Fair and Cattle Show would be held in Brighton every October from 1816 into the mid-1830s.

Recognizing that the selection of Brighton for this important agricultural gathering would benefit the local economy, the town's Board of Selectmen readily agreed to the organization's request for "permanent regulations to secure order" and an "accommodation of land" on which to lay out their fairgrounds and construct an exhibition hall.

The town fathers took extraordinary care in selecting the site for these facilities. Samuel Wyllys Pomeroy, owner of the Bull's Head Tavern, a hostelry that stood a quarter of a mile east of Brighton Center, was so anxious to have the fair located near his establishment that he offered the MSPA the use of ten acres of land on the opposite side of Washington Street for a fair ground (the area now crossed by Snow and Shannon Streets).

But Brighton's Selectmen rejected Pomeroy's offer, noting that "as every eye has been directed to a field owned by Mr. A[biel] Winship fronting the public house as being the most eligible situation," they would do their best to secure that property.

The Winship parcel lay on the crest of the hill on which the Winship Elementary School now stands. The town's leaders had little difficulty persuading the public-spirited Winship, the oldest son of the founder of the local cattle industry, to place this acreage at the disposal of the agricultural society.

Here we see Agricultural Hall at its present location in Brighton Center. *Photo by William P. Marchione.*

Part of the attraction of this elevation—thereafter called Agricultural Hill—was its proximity to the largest public house in Brighton, Hastings Tavern, which sat across Washington Street, just east of the present-day Parsons Street intersection. In addition, the town's largest meeting hall—the sanctuary of the First Parish Church—stood but a short distance away at the northeast corner of Washington and Market Streets.

Scientific farming was making great headway in Massachusetts in the early 1800s through the efforts of the MSPA. Though the society's offices were situated in Boston, the focal point of its public activities in these years was its annual Brighton Fair and Cattle Show, which the society's official history notes, "embraced everything that could interest a farmer or be of benefit to agriculture; and in connection with them the importation of superior breeds of farm animals laid a firm and scientific base for the excellence which developed later."

Weeks before the October fair was due to open, display items began arriving at Agricultural Hall. The two-story structure, measuring seventy by thirty-six feet, stood on "beautiful and elevated grounds." Its first floor was used to display the latest farm implements as well as prize-winning fruit and vegetables, while the second story accommodated textile and handicraft exhibits. In addition, cattle pens were laid out on either side of the building, where prize livestock were displayed and plowing matches and other competitive activities were held on the nearby slopes of the hill.

The fair always began with a procession from Agricultural Hall to the First Church, where the minister (the Reverend John Foster before 1827, and the Reverend Daniel Austin thereafter) invoked God's blessing on the occasion.

Awards were then announced by the various committees. In 1829 prizes and premiums were awarded in the following categories: fat cattle, bulls and bull calves, cows and heifers, sheep and swine, inventions, butter and cheese, cider, grain and vegetables, plowing and manufacturing. A seventeen-pound turnip, a nineteen-pound radish, and a bough on which pears hung like a cluster of grapes were among the outstanding exhibits of that year.

After the distribution of these awards and of the various premiums a sumptuous meal was served at Hastings Tavern (or at the much larger Cattle Fair Hotel after 1830) and speeches were heard on various agricultural topics.

One of the most eagerly anticipated features of these annual banquets was the presentation of toasts by prominent participants. Those presenting toasts in 1835 included U.S. Senator Daniel Webster, noted orator Edward Everett, the great industrialist Abbott Lawrence and U.S. Supreme Court Justice Joseph Story.

By the mid-1830s, the Brighton Fair and Cattle Show was in decline owing, in part at least, "to the effects of counter attractions by the county societies," according to an MSPA history.

The most important factor in explaining the discontinuance of the Brighton fairs, however, was the building of the Boston and Worcester Railroad, completed in 1835, which shifted the geographical center of the state's agricultural economy westward, making Brighton relatively inconvenient for the fair's patrons.

Having stood unused for some years, in 1844 the land on which the Brighton Fair and Cattle Show had been held for more than two decades was subdivided and sold at public auction. It was at this time that Agricultural Hall was moved off the hill to its present location in Brighton Center and converted into a hotel called the Eastern Market Hotel, so named because it stood just east of the Brighton Stockyards.

The historic structure continued to serve as a hotel until the late 1880s, one of six hotels in Brighton Center accommodating the farmers, drovers and cattle dealers who frequented the Brighton Cattle Market. After 1875, the building was purchased by Dodenah Scates, and its name was changed to the Scates Hotel. The hotel closed in the 1880s, following the 1884 removal of the Brighton Stockyards to North Brighton.

Agricultural Hall thereafter housed a variety of enterprises and the building experienced substantial alteration, losing much of its original architectural detailing.

Thanks to Steve Wasserman's restoration work, however, Agricultural Hall (the oldest and most historic building in Brighton Center) now has an appearance far more suggestive of its historic character and function.

8

NOAH WORCESTER
Brighton's Apostle of Peace

A historical marker at 437 Washington Street, at the site of his former residence, identifies Noah Worcester merely as Brighton's first postmaster. But Noah Worcester was much more than a simple village postmaster. He was also a distinguished Unitarian clergyman, the co-founder of the American peace movement and the author of *A Solemn Review of the Custom of War*, the first significant work of American pacifism, described by one historian as "an epoch-making classic in the history of peace literature."

According to historian Peter Brock, author of *Radical Pacifists in Antebellum America*, Dr. Noah Worcester of Brighton and David Low Dodge of New York were "the real founders of the American peace movement, each at the beginning working independently without knowledge of the other."

Noah Worcester was born in Hollis, New Hampshire, in 1758, the eldest son of Noah Worcester, Esq., "a prominent farmer of an active and energetic mind" who would later help write the New Hampshire state constitution.

Noah received little formal schooling. At the outbreak of the American Revolution, the sixteen-year-old marched off with his father's company of New Hampshire militiamen to join the Patriot army, then massing at Cambridge. A few weeks later Worcester experienced war for the first time at the battle of Bunker Hill, where he barely escaped death. He also fought in the bloody 1777 battle of Bennington. Of the latter episode he would write that he "felt much worse in going over the ground the next day than during engagement itself." The carnage he witnessed on both of these

Revolutionary War battlefields helped mold the pacifist convictions to which he would later give eloquent expression in *A Solemn Review of the Custom of War* and on the pages of the pacifist journal *The Friend of Peace*.

In 1778 at age twenty, the young veteran returned to his native state, where he married Hannah Brown and settled eventually in Thornton, New Hampshire, in the mountainous north central part of the state. Here he supported his growing family through a combination of school teaching and shoemaking. The rural schoolmaster also subjected himself to a course of vigorous mental discipline. As one commentator noted, Worcester "always had his pen in hand to note down every thought that occurred to him."

It was Reverend Selden Church of Compton, New Hampshire, who first suggested to Worcester that he should become a preacher of the Gospel, with the result that the young man submitted to examination by the local ministerial association, and in 1786 was granted a license to preach.

The members of the Thornton Congregational Church soon after elected him minister. Worcester served this tiny White Mountain community during the almost quarter-century that followed as minister, schoolmaster, selectman, town clerk, justice of the peace and state legislator, while supplementing his small ministerial salary through a combination of farming, shoemaking, teaching and itinerant preaching as an agent for the New Hampshire Missionary Society.

Left: Noah Worcester, the nation's leading pacifist, known as "the Apostle of Peace," resided in Brighton from 1813 until his death in 1837, and served as the town's first postmaster. *Courtesy of the Brighton-Allston Historical Society Archives.*

Opposite: The Noah Worcester house stood at the northwest corner of Washington and Foster Streets. It was in this house, in 1813, that Worcester wrote his most important work, the antiwar tract, *A Solemn Review of the Custom of War.*
Courtesy of the Brighton-Allston Historical Society Archives.

In 1810, however, Worcester relocated to the more southerly town of Salisbury, New Hampshire, to assist his brother, Reverend Thomas Worcester, who had been incapacitated by illness. It was while living in Salisbury that he wrote his first book, *Bible News of the Father, Son, and Holy Ghost*, a vigorous defense of the central tenets of the Unitarian creed. This led to an "earnest controversy" with the Congregationalist Hopkington Association, of which he had long been a member, which condemned him as an apostate. Having alienated the religious right of his day, however, the New Hampshire minister immediately became the darling of the religious left.

Worcester's spirited and closely reasoned defense of Unitarianism had attracted the attention of a group of Boston-area clergymen that included such eminent figures as William Ellery Channing of Boston's Federal Street Church and John Lowell of Boston's West Church. These religious liberals were about to establish a publication to defend their point of view, called *The Christian Disciple*. Worcester was offered the editorship of this journal, which he eagerly accepted.

Why did Noah Worcester choose Brighton rather than Boston as a place of residence? Boston was the focal point of the religious controversies of the day. His Brighton residence, by contrast, offered few advantages, situated as it was adjacent to the crowded and noisy Brighton Cattle Market.

Worcester's decision to locate in Brighton rather than Boston was probably taken as an economy measure. His salary as editor of *The Christian Disciple* was meager. Lacking an independent source of income, he lived essentially from hand to mouth. Indicative of his poverty is the fact that he never owned the Washington Street house that he occupied for the last twenty-four years of his life, but rented it from Gorham Parsons, the owner of the adjacent Oakland Farms estate.

Despite the sometimes inconvenient conditions under which he lived, Noah Worcester's years in Brighton were by far the most productive of his life.

Events of great historical interest transpired in Worcester's Brighton residence. Here the liberal clergyman edited, from 1813 to 1819, *The Friend of Peace*, one of the most influential religious publications of the day. Here, in 1814 (at the low point of American fortunes in the War of 1812), he penned his celebrated pacifist tract, *A Solemn Review of the Custom of War*, thereby inaugurating the American peace movement. Here he helped to found the Massachusetts Peace Society, the oldest such organization in the nation, which he served faithfully as secretary for many years.

Noah Worcester was presented with a number of honorary degrees by New England colleges in recognition of his contributions to theology and reform during his years in Brighton, including a master's degree from Dartmouth and a doctorate from Harvard, the latter conferred in 1818.

In 1817 Noah Worcester received an appointment from the federal government as postmaster of Brighton, though the actual work of sorting and tending to the mail was apparently performed by his unmarried daughter, Sally. Thus the Worcester House, cradle of the American peace movement, also served as Brighton's first post office.

What manner of man was Noah Worcester? The Reverend George Blagden, minister of Brighton Center's Evangelical Congregational Church, remembered Worcester as physically imposing, but also mild-mannered. Worcester stood over six feet in height and was large-framed, Blagden recalled, and wore his hair long, under a broad-brimmed hat. He carried a staff, and usually dressed in a roomy black gown.

> *His habits of living were very simple, partly, I have no doubt, from taste and partly from necessity; for I have always understood that his means were quite limited…I seem to see him and hear him now—an unusually kind and meek and modest but courageous and conscientious old man.*

Dr. Channing, a close associate for many years, remembered Worcester for his gentleness of spirit and great intellectual curiosity. "On leaving [the Worcester] house and turning my face towards the city," noted Channing, "I have said how much richer is this poor man than the richest who dwell yonder."

Noah Worcester, Brighton's celebrated "Apostle of Peace," died in his Washington Street home on October 31, 1837. Funeral services were held at Brighton's First Church, of which he had been a member since 1813, and he was laid to rest in the Market Street Burying Ground. In 1838, however, the organizers of the newly established Mount Auburn Cemetery furnished a free seventy-square-foot burial plot for the celebrated pacifist, whereupon his remains were moved to Mount Auburn in Cambridge.

In 1914 the Society for the Preservation of New England Antiquities considered adding the Worcester House to its growing collection of house museums, but finally decided against the acquisition. After its demolition, the SPNEA Bulletin noted, somewhat superciliously,

> the house was of interest mainly from the point of view of Brighton (as the home of Noah Worcester and the first post office), and local people and local patriotic societies should have preserved it. The loss is chiefly theirs and no future building however fine can ever give them back what they lost in the Worcester house.

9

James L.L.F. Warren of Brighton
"The Father of California Agriculture"

Bostonians have made many significant contributions to the development of California and the Pacific Northwest. Between 1790 and 1792, a Boston-owned ship, the *Columbia*, was the first American vessel to visit the Pacific Northwest, the name of the great Columbia River deriving from its explorations. So common was the arrival of Boston-owned trading vessels in western waters by the early 1800s, that Americans were referred to simply as "Boston Men," whether from the Hub or not. Later, Bostonians also played a key role in the development of the western mining industry and in the financing and management of the transcontinental railroad, the first reliable east-west transit link.

Another major contribution to western history that deserves to be much better known was that of a Brighton horticulturalist, James L.L.F. Warren, who has been referred to as the "Father of California Agriculture."

James Lloyd Lafayette Warren was born in the Boston suburb of Brighton on August 12, 1805, the son of Captain Joseph Warren, carpenter, farmer and a longtime Brighton town clerk. James's childhood residence stood atop the eastern slope of Nonantum Hill, on the site of the present EF Language Institute on Lake Street. Later he resided in a house that is still standing at 222 Lake Street.

From an early age Warren showed a great interest in the cultivation of plants and flowers. As early as 1820, when he was just fifteen, a nursery he laid out on his family's Brighton estate on the western side of Lake Street opposite present-day Rogers Park, was attracting wide notice from horticultural enthusiasts. By 1829, this establishment, the Nonantum Vale Gardens, was a famed and thriving enterprise.

James Lloyd Lafayette Warren, the Brighton horticulturalist who immigrated to California in 1850 and became the "Father of California Agriculture." *Courtesy of the Brighton-Allston Historical Society Archives.*

Warren also won many awards from the Massachusetts State Board of Agriculture for his contributions to horticulture. In 1838 he received a medal from the Boston Horticultural Society for growing the first tomatoes in Massachusetts. He also propagated new varieties of the camellia, which he later introduced into Britain and California.

Warren was also a highly successful Boston businessman, the owner of two enterprises in the downtown area. In 1826 he founded a dry goods emporium, known as Warren's Shawl and Silk Store, in the Joy Building on Washington Street near the Old State House. More significant still was his founding in 1844 of Warren's Floral Saloon, an exhibition hall and salesroom in the Tremont Temple building. He inaugurated this downtown horticultural outlet with an exhibit of a bed of tulips (then still a rarity in the United States) that was nine feet wide by one hundred feet long.

Warren's Brighton nursery and downtown "floral saloon" attracted many distinguished visitors over the years, including such political and literary luminaries as Henry Clay, Daniel Webster, John C. Calhoun, Wendell Phillips, Ralph Waldo Emerson, Nathaniel P. Willis, William Cullen Bryant, John Greenleaf Whittier and Henry Wadsworth Longfellow, to name but a few.

The great horticulturalist's career also had its journalistic, educational, political, diplomatic and philanthropic dimensions. The common denominator of virtually all his activities was human and societal improvement.

Warren's commitment to reform included a leadership role in the Massachusetts branch of the Liberty Party, a radical antislavery political movement that his close friend, the poet William Cullen Bryant, helped found in 1839.

In 1846 Warren, who was at the point of sailing for Europe, was enlisted by the State Department to carry dispatches to George Bancroft, U.S. Minister to Great Britain (possibly relating to the Oregon dispute which was then troubling Anglo-American relations). He remained in Europe for two years, traveling extensively in the British Isles, France and the Low Countries. He also toured Ireland, then in the grips of the devastating potato famine.

Upon his return to the United States, Warren called attention to the "intense suffering [and] the absolute starvation of thousands" in Ireland, joining others, including the great Irish temperance lecturer Father Theobald Mathew and the so-called Learned Blacksmith Elihu Burritt, in proposing a plan for Irish famine relief. The U.S. government became interested in their proposal, and soon after supplied the U.S. frigate *Jamestown* to transport food to the famine victims.

U.S. acquisition of California in 1848 and the discovery of gold at Sutter's Mill in the same year led to large-scale migration of easterners, the

The residence of James L.L.F. Warren still stands at 202 Lake Street, Brighton. His ten-acre nursery, Nonantum Vale Gardens, extended from the house in a northerly direction toward Washington Street. *Photo by William P. Marchione.*

so-called forty-niners, to the western El Dorado. One of these was Warren, who was destined to spend the rest of his life in California.

While most of the forty-niners were young, unmarried men, at the time of his migration Warren was a mature forty-four, a married man and the father of several children. Moreover, his decision to go west was a carefully thought out business decision. Warren had accepted an offer from a group of Boston and New York investors to act as business manager of the recently organized Sweden Mining Company. In exchange for their passage to California, the participants agreed to work in the gold fields under company auspices for an established period of time.

Warren set out on March 2, 1849, for California, temporarily leaving his family behind in Boston. The members of the Sweden Mining Company were transported to the gold fields aboard a company-owned vessel, the *Sweden*, a 650-ton ship of recent construction, named in honor of the great Swedish soprano Jenny Lind, a popular favorite in Boston. The ship, with its 212 passengers, reached San Francisco by way of Cape Horn on August 6, 1849, after a torturous five-month journey.

Warren had scant opportunity to demonstrate his skills as a mining company manager, however, for the employees of the Sweden Company quickly reneged on their agreements, scattering to the various gold fields on an individual basis.

Never easily discouraged, Warren saw other business opportunities in California and proceeded to take advantage of them. He quickly established a letter-carrying service between San Francisco and the interior mining camps. And in November 1849, a mere three months after his arrival, founded a general provisioning firm, Warren and Company, in California's capital city of Sacramento.

The frequency of scurvy in the mining camps and his own deep interest in horticulture led Warren to orient his provisioning business toward the acquisition and sale of fruit trees, seeds and agricultural implements. By 1852 Warren's store had become so important to the state's expanding agricultural economy that it served as the site of the first California State Fair, the rooms above it being dubbed Agricultural Hall, possibly in imitation of the Brighton facility of the same name.

Many of the practices followed at this first California State Fair, which Warren almost single-handedly organized, closely paralleled those followed at the Brighton Fair and Cattle Show, held for many years at Brighton's Agricultural Hall under the auspices of the Massachusetts Society for Promoting Agriculture. Here again we see additional evidence of the influence of New England men, practices and institutions upon the west.

In 1853 Warren shifted his business headquarters to San Francisco, the state's largest city, thereafter running the enterprise in association with his son, John Quincy Adams Warren.

Warren's contributions to California agriculture were many and varied. In addition to his role as initiator of the first state fair, Warren was also largely responsible for establishing the principal agricultural publication in the west, *The California Farmer and Journal of Useful Sciences*, and also took the lead in the foundation of the California State Agricultural Society, which was incorporated, largely at his behest, by the state legislature in 1854, with permission to establish two experimental farms and to erect meeting halls and exhibition buildings.

As historian Walton Bean wrote of this Brighton horticulturalist's many contributions to California agriculture:

> *One of the greatest needs of the frontier state's slowly and clumsily developing agriculture was the introduction and adaptation of new crops, and it was here that Warren rendered one of the greatest of his services. His office served as a clearinghouse for the exchange of information, specimens, and seeds, not merely within California, but with other parts of the United States, South America, and the Orient.*

10

Brighton's Historic Nonantum Valley

In the late nineteenth century, more than twenty ponds dotted the landscape of Allston-Brighton. Today, only one remains, Chandler's Pond. This twelve-acre sheet of water, now part of the Alice Gallagher Park, is one of the community's most attractive visual and recreational amenities.

Chandler's Pond lies in the so-called Nonantum Valley, which is enclosed by Nonantum Hill to the north and Waban Hill to the south. The pond was excavated for ice-making purposes by local horticulturalist and landowner William C. Strong in 1855.

Chandler's Pond is fed by Dana Brook, which flows out of Newton. After leaving the Nonantum Valley this watercourse meanders more than a mile in a more or less northeasterly direction before emptying into the Charles River in the vicinity of the Soldier's Field Road Extension. The portion of the waterway below the pond is now completely submerged in conduits.

The Nonantum Valley itself has a fascinating history. In October 1646, the Reverend John Eliot, minister of Roxbury, discussed in the first chapter, performed his first conversions of Native Americans to Christianity at the western end of this valley. The leader of the natives was Waban, the man after whom the hill was named. A Praying Indian community was immediately established on the site by Eliot, and given the name "Nonantum," which meant "rejoicing" in the Algonquian language. A monument, off Eliot Memorial Road in Newton, marks the site of Nonantum, the oldest Christian Indian community in British North America.

The land on which Chandler's Pond is now situated was first owned by Richard Dana, the American founder of a family that would later produce many notable statesmen, writers and reformers. The Dana family owned this acreage more or less continuously until the early nineteenth century. Their homestead, which stood in Brighton's Oak Square, at the corner of Nonantum and Washington Streets, was destroyed by fire in the 1870s.

By 1837 the southern part of the Dana property had passed into the hands of Horace Gray, an influential Boston businessman and horticulturalist who played a key role in the foundation of the Boston Public Garden. Gray's imposing country residence stood at the crest of Nonantum Hill, overlooking the valley in which Chandler's Pond would later be created. According to one account, Gray

> *erected on the grounds the largest grape houses known in the United States, in which were grown extensively numerous varieties of foreign grapes. For the testing of these under glass in cold houses,* [he] *erected a large curvilinear-roof house, two hundred feet long and twenty-four wide. This was such a success that he built two more of the same dimension.*

In 1848, however, financial losses forced Gray to sell his Brighton property. The purchaser was William C. Strong, who soon expanded the horticultural business there by laying out additional vines and adding other plants. Strong also built an immense greenhouse for his Nonantum Valley Nurseries, where "under one continuous roof of glass of 18,000 square feet, is an enclosure where plants are grown in the open ground; [in which] immense quantities of roses and flowers are daily cut for the market." A much-acclaimed horticulturalist, Strong served as president of the Massachusetts Horticultural Society from 1871 to 1874.

As previously noted, it was Strong who excavated Chandler's Pond in 1855 for ice-cutting. In 1865 he created a second pond for ice-cutting, just west of Chandler's, called Strong's Pond, which has since disappeared.

Kenrick Street was put through in 1856 on the northern margin of Chandler's Pond. The oldest house on the street, number 54, almost certainly belonged to an early employee of the ice-cutting operation. Two icehouses were built adjacent to these bodies of water. One stood at the corner of Lake and Kenrick Streets; the other between the two ponds (on the site now occupied by the Chandler's Pond Apartments).

Strong first leased and then, in 1858, sold the more easterly of the ponds to Malcolm Chandler, an experienced ice merchant who had previously operated an ice-cutting establishment on Hammond Pond in Newton. Soon after this purchase Chandler built an imposing Greek Revival–style mansion for himself at 70 Lake Street, overlooking the valley, a building that still exists.

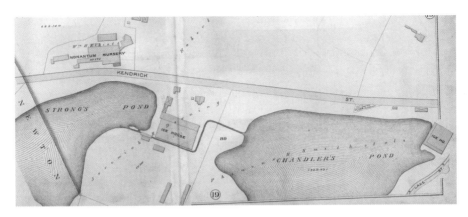

An 1890 map showing the two ice-cutting ponds that William C. Strong excavated between 1855 and 1865, and their adjacent icehouses, as well as Strong's neighboring Nonantum Nursery. *Courtesy of the Brighton-Allston Historical Society Archives.*

Here we see the more westerly of the icehouses, which Strong built following the excavation of his second pond in 1865, and which was later owned by J.R. Downing. *Courtesy of the Brighton-Allston Historical Society Archives.*

William Chamberlain Strong, the noted Brighton horticulturalist and entrepreneur, who served as president of the Massachusetts Horticultural Society in the early 1870s. *Courtesy of the Brighton-Allston Historical Society Archives.*

Strong continued ice-cutting at the more westerly pond until 1880. Once refrigeration was introduced in the early 1870s, however, a fierce competition developed between the two ice-cutters for the remaining business in natural ice. Following a destructive fire at Strong's icehouse in 1872, Chandler (who was already experiencing serious financial difficulties) was arrested and charged with arson. However, the namesake of Chandler's Pond was eventually found innocent of the crime.

In 1880 Strong sold his Brighton ice-cutting interests to Jeremiah Downing. Long interested in real estate development, Strong had in 1875 moved to Beacon Street in Newton's Auburndale section where he developed a new suburb, called Waban, after the local Indian leader.

Downing continued cutting ice on Strong's Pond into the early years of the twentieth century. In 1895, however, he sold much of his acreage to the organizers of the Chestnut Hill Country Club. A founding member of the Massachusetts Golf Association, this country club would be redesigned in the 1920s by the nation's leading golf course architect, Donald Ross.

By the 1920s, the former Strong icehouse and its outbuildings had been converted into horse auction stables, owned first by the Pickens family and later by J.C. Keith. One commentator has described Brighton's Keith Stables as the mecca of the New England horse trade in the 1930s and '40s: "The barn had accommodations for 500 horses and feed during the 1940s…Five carloads of horses arrived weekly by rail from the mid-west for all-day Wednesday auctions at Keith's." In the late 1940s, the Keith Stables and many of its horses were destroyed in a spectacular fire.

Meanwhile, in 1883 Chandler's Pond had been acquired by Phineas B. Smith, the owner of the Jamaica Pond Ice Company in Jamaica Plain. Smith had held a mortgage on the Chandler property since 1871. When the Chandlers' heirs (Malcolm having died in the mid-1870s) failed to meet the mortgage payments, Smith seized the property. Ice-cutting on Chandler's Pond did not outlast the century, however. In 1897 the large icehouse at the corner of Lake and Kenrick Streets was destroyed by fire.

In 1913 Chandler's Pond passed into the hands of the Roman Catholic Archdiocese of Boston. The pond had long since become a popular place of resort for skaters. Students at neighboring St. John's Seminary also made good use of the frozen surface during winter. As Brighton native George G. Ryan reminisced of skating at Chandler's Pond in a recent *Boston Pilot* article:

> *Ever since the hey-day of ice-harvesting, Chandler's Pond has been in constant winter use as an outdoor skating rink, a place of recreation for the easterly Newtons, the whole of Allston-Brighton, and even Chestnut*

Hill...Because it was so still, Chandler's Pond was better for skating than the Charles River, which flowed seaward just fast enough to ripple the surface and discourage the quick freeze so characteristic of Chandler's. Moreover, the tiny pond lacked the river's depth, a definite plus should the ice thin, thaw, and crack, thereby threatening skaters with an unscheduled dip.

In 1925 the archdiocese sold the pond and the surrounding acreage to developer George W. Robertson, who proceeded to subdivide the land into lots for residential development. There was even some talk at this juncture of filling the pond. Lake Shore Road on the southern rim was put through in the mid-twenties. By the early 1930s, the margin of the pond was largely developed.

The City of Boston acquired the Chandler's Pond acreage from various owners in the late 1930s, some of it apparently in lieu of unpaid real estate taxes. In 1941, at the urging of Boston City Council member Maurice Sullivan, the city established the Alice Gallagher Park on the southern and western rim of the pond, naming it in memory of the recently deceased wife of former City Council member Edward Gallagher. Councilor Gallagher had played a key role in the city's acquisition of the property.

11

OF HORTICULTURE
AND ANTISLAVERY
The Kenricks of Newton

In the early nineteenth century Greater Boston stood at the forefront of horticultural enterprise in the United States, as evidenced by the foundation of the Massachusetts Horticultural Society in 1829, and the laying out by that organization of Cambridge's elaborately planted Mount Auburn Cemetery in 1831.

But the beginnings of horticulture as a business enterprise (as distinguished from a gentleman's avocation) goes back much further—to the 1790s and to the highly interesting figure of John Kenrick of Newton.

John Kenrick (1755–1833) launched his career in 1790 as a purveyor of plants and trees (primarily the latter), when he laid out several rows of peach stones on his estate on the southwestern slope of Nonantum Hill in Newton near the present Newton-Brighton boundary. Brighton's Kenrick Street was named in his memory.

So successful were his early experiments in pomology, that in 1794 Kenrick founded a commercial nursery, offering the buying public as many varieties of fruit-bearing trees and bushes as were then available in the Boston area. In 1797 the pioneer horticulturalist added ornamental trees to his stock, including two acres of Lombardy poplars, then the most salable tree in this part of the country. Kenrick also aggressively imported foreign varieties of fruit-bearing trees and bushes, until his Nonantum Hill nursery became the most extensive and varied establishment of its kind in the New England region.

The Kenricks had long been a leading Newton family. Their American progenitor, John Kenrick I, settled in the town in 1658, having purchased

Anno Domini 1843

1843.

Descriptive Catalogue.

NURSERY OF WILLIAM KENRICK,

NONANTUM HILL, IN NEWTON,

(NEAR BOSTON.)

THE

ABRIDGED DESCRIPTIVE CATALOGUE

OF

FRUIT AND HARDY ORNAMENTAL TREES, SHRUBS, ROSES, HERBACEOUS PLANTS, &C.,

WHICH ARE

THERE CULTIVATED AND FOR SALE.

For the Year 1843.

A VERY LIBERAL DISCOUNT WILL BE MADE ON THE PRICES, WHERE A LARGE QUANTITY IS DESIRED.

A Kenrick Nurseries catalog for the year 1843. The Kenrick establishment was the oldest horticultural business in Massachusetts, founded in the mid-1790s, and lay just over the town boundary in Newton. Brighton's Kenrick Street leads to the site of this pioneer nursery. *From the author's personal collection.*

280 "broad and tangled acres" on the banks of the Charles River opposite Needham in the present Oak Hill section. Here the future horticulturalist was born in 1755.

In 1775 John Kenrick acquired the acreage in the eastern part of Newton on which he later established his famous nursery—land that had previously belonged to the prominent Durant family. This estate occupied a site of great historical importance, for it was here in 1646 that the Reverend John Eliot of Roxbury, the Apostle to the Indians, had established the Praying Indian village of Nonantum. The estate's 1732 mansion house—now known as the Durant-Kenrick House—still stands on Newton's Waverly Avenue.

Horticulturalist John Kenrick proved himself a pioneer of a different kind in 1817 when he published a fifty-nine-page booklet entitled *The Horrors of Slavery*, which lashed out at American society for its hypocrisy in sustaining an institution that contravened the principles upon which the American republic had been founded.

The antislavery movement was in its infancy when this angry tract made its appearance. Kenrick was venturing on dangerous ground in embracing abolitionism. The great majority of Northerners regarded slavery as a strictly local concern, which no resident of a free state had any business raising. Kenrick was, in fact, a decade and a half ahead of his time in advocating freedom for the slaves. As one commentator noted: "Wendell Phillips and William Lloyd Garrison were [then still] school-boys, and John Brown was a lad tanning hides in Ohio."

While *The Horrors of Slavery* contained very little that was original—it primarily consists of excerpts from the works of earlier writers—the intensity of the author's antislavery convictions are powerfully evident in his fiery and eloquent introduction.

> [Is it not] *incredible* [he queried] *that a people, so jealous of their natural rights, could hold in the most absolute and degrading servitude, under a free government, a million of fellow beings, who have by nature, reason and justice, as fair a claim to liberty as themselves? Could it be supposed that a people, thus jealous of their own rights, could treat their brethren of a different colour as property, to be bought and sold like oxen and horses! Yet such is the inconsistency of the white inhabitants of the United States—a people who call themselves Christians!*
>
> *The compiler firmly believes that his countrymen stand exposed to the righteous rebukes of Providence for this glaring inconsistency and inhumanity; that whether they shall be tried at the bar of reason, the bar of conscience, or the bar of God, they may justly be condemned out of their own mouths; and that all their arguments, and all their fightings for liberty,*

may be produced as evidence, that, as a people they do unto others as they would not that others should do unto them.

Kenrick's nursery continued to flourish, despite the stance that he took on the controversial slavery issue. In 1823 the *New England Farmer*, the leading agricultural paper of the day, described the Kenrick nursery as "the finest in America." In addition to its fruit and ornamental trees, by the 1820s it included extensive grounds devoted to the cultivation of red currants, from which Kenrick was producing large quantities of wine—some 3,600 gallons in 1826 alone. Clearly, the temperance crusade, which was just then emerging as a force in American life, had less appeal to the Newton reformer than abolitionism.

By the early 1830s there were two Kenrick nurseries on the Nonantum Hill property, for John's eldest son, William, had established a separate enterprise on an adjoining parcel. In 1833, however, when his father died, the two nurseries were united under William's capable management.

William Kenrick (1789–1872) was a perhaps even more influential horticulturalist than his father. A founding member of the Massachusetts Horticultural Society, William sat on that organization's governing council from 1829 to 1841, and was long the leading member of its standing committee on fruit trees and fruit.

The variety of fruit-bearing trees that William Kenrick offered the public at his Nonantum Hill nursery is truly impressive. By 1832, when he issued his first catalog, he was able to list, in addition to 148 varieties of apples, 155 of pears, 99 of peaches, 48 of cherries and 47 of plums. And the number mounted steadily with the passage of time. By 1838, varieties of apple trees had risen to 228, while that of pears rose to an amazing 317.

So important were Kenrick's contributions to pomology that in 1835 the Massachusetts Horticultural Society presented him with a special award for his "successful efforts at procuring scions of new fruits from Europe, and for his valuable treatise on fruit trees."

William Kenrick authored two important horticultural works: *The New American Orchardist* (1833), which went through seven editions, and *The American Silk Grower's Guide* (1835), reflecting his absorbing interest in silk culture and the raising of mulberry trees.

But William Kenrick's activities were not limited to horticulture any more than his father's. He also detested slavery. A series of letters that William wrote his friend, U.S. Representative Horace Mann (also a resident of Newton), during the North-South crisis of 1849–50, attest to his deep convictions on the slavery issue. These letters, which now reside in the Horace Mann papers in the Massachusetts Historical Society, show the horticulturalist to have been a firm opponent of sectional compromise.

He strongly supported the Wilmot Proviso (which sought the exclusion of slavery from the territories) whatever the consequences might be.

> *And now I beseech* [Kenrick wrote Mann on March 12, 1850], *if it be possible, let us have the wholesome and wholesale Wilmot Proviso…I am persuaded it can and will be done. If not, I would prefer that things take their own way without any compromise, with no legislation at all. If God sees fit to inflict any more slavery on us—be it so—until the measure of the iniquity of slavery is full. God can, as he has oft done, abolish slavery, in his own good time, in more ways than one, and will.*

While William Kenrick retired from the horticultural business in 1856, he continued to be interested in horticulture and in national affairs until his death in 1876. His withdrawal from active business did not, however, lead to the demise of the Kenrick Nursery on Nonantum Hill, which continued to be operated by brother John A. Kenrick for some years under the name Nonantum Dale Gardens.

12

THE NAME ALLSTON
An Appropriate Choice?

Boston's Allston section is said to be the only community in the United States named for an artist—the great Romantic painter Washington Allston (1779–1843). This is, of course, no small distinction.

But who was Washington Allston and how did his name come to be applied to this Boston suburb? And why was the painter Allston honored rather than some other Boston-area artist of perhaps equal distinction such as Copley, Stuart or Trumbull?

The choice of the name Allston is especially surprising when one considers that this painter was not a native of New England. Allston was born in distant South Carolina into a wealthy family of slave-owning rice planters. Though he came to New England at a fairly young age to prepare to enter Harvard College, much of his life was spent (his most artistically productive period) in Europe. By the time he settled permanently in Boston in 1818, the painter was already forty years of age, and most of his significant work was behind him.

Another factor that renders the choice somewhat surprising, perhaps even inappropriate, was the scant interest this painter paid American subject matter. Apart from a few portraits of family members and friends, Allston painted almost nothing on American themes. Not one of his brilliant marine paintings, stunningly iridescent landscapes or elaborately executed history paintings celebrates the American experience.

While Copley and Stuart have left us a wonderful record in portraiture of early American history; while John Trumbull created giant history canvasses celebrating our Revolutionary and early national history; while Thomas

Cole and his Hudson River school associates captured the wilder image of our primeval landscape on their canvases, Allston preferred dealing with Neoclassical and religious subject matter, considering American themes somewhat inferior. While he painted brilliantly in a broad range of genres, as evidenced by such stunning canvasses as *The Rising of a Thunderstorm at Sea* (1804), *Moonlit Landscape* (1819) and *Elijah in the Desert* (1818), in no real sense—apart from his birth and periods of residence here—can he be classified as an American painter.

So how did Allston's name come to be applied to the eastern half of the Town of Brighton?

The name Allston was chosen as an address for a new post office that the federal government had decided to open in that section of the town of Brighton. On February 11, 1868, local residents gathered in the Boston and Worcester Railroad depot at Cambridge Crossing, as this section of Brighton was then known. After prolonged and indecisive discussion the participants adopted a suggestion of Reverend Frederic Augustus Whitney that the name Allston be adopted as a local postal address.

Reverend Whitney, who was the minister of Brighton's First Church (Unitarian), a resident of Gardner Street and a highly respected figure, was said to have recommended the name because Allston had once lived across the river in nearby Cambridgeport and also because Brighton had, before 1807, formed a part of the Town of Cambridge.

It is quite possible (even probable) that Whitney knew Allston personally, for the future minister had attended Harvard College and the Harvard Theological Seminary in the early 1830s during the time when Allston lived in Cambridgeport. Harvard students often visited the painter's studio near Central Square to examine the giant canvases and other works of art that he had on display there.

How appropriate then was the choice of the name Allston for the Boston suburb that bears its name? While it may not have been the very best choice in historic terms, it was in many ways an understandable choice.

Though Allston settled in the Boston area at a late stage of his life, he had long considered himself a New Englander. His association with the region dated back to 1787 when his parents sent the then-eight-year-old boy to live with a maternal uncle in Newport, Rhode Island, in order, it was said, that his "nervous...organization might be recruited by a more bracing air," and also so that he might be adequately prepared for admission to Harvard College.

From 1796 to 1800 the handsome Southerner formed lifelong friendships at Harvard with members of Boston's social elite. He would eventually marry into two leading Boston-area families: the Channings and the Danas.

The great painter Washington Allston, the leading American artist of his day, who resided in neighboring Cambridgeport toward the end of his life. In 1868 his name was applied to the eastern part of Brighton as a postal address. *Courtesy of the Brighton-Allston Historical Society Archives.*

His native South, by contrast, held little appeal for Allston. He returned there only once, to collect his inheritance.

Upon graduation from Harvard in 1800, Allston left immediately for Europe, the center of the artistic world of his day, remaining there for most of the next two decades. He returned to Boston in 1808, married Ann Channing, the sister of the Reverend William Ellery Channing, but was back in London by 1811.

Once Allston returned to America permanently in 1818, he chose to live in Boston. During the last quarter century of his life (1818 to 1843) he resided first in the Hub (off Federal Street) and then in the nearby suburb of Cambridgeport.

Had the painter not settled in Cambridgeport in 1830, it is unlikely that his name would have been given to the eastern part of Brighton. His second marriage (his first wife had died in 1815) to Martha Remington Dana prompted his removal from Boston to the developing suburb on the banks of the Charles, directly across the river from present-day Allston. The Danas were a leading Cambridge family. Martha's grandfather, Francis Dana, Congressman and first American minister to Russia, had been the principal developer of Cambridgeport. Allston's father-in-law was a literary figure of importance and professor at Harvard as well as Allston's closest friend in the last years of his life.

In Cambridgeport the Allstons first lived in a house situated about a third of a mile south of Central Square, with an excellent view of the Charles River marshes. In 1831 the painter built a studio at the corner of present-day Magazine and Auburn Streets, which he designed himself. Shaped like a Greek temple, this edifice was about twenty by forty feet long, large enough to house the giant paintings that were his stock in trade. Later the couple moved to a house at 172 Auburn Street, much closer to his "painting room," as he called his studio. The leading literary and artistic figures of the day—in the era when Boston was the Athens of America—visited Allston in his Cambridgeport studio: Henry Wadsworth Longfellow, Thomas Sully, Ralph Waldo Emerson, Washington Irving, Margaret Fuller, William Ellery Channing, Nathaniel Hawthorne, James Russell Lowell and Oliver Wendell Holmes, just to name a few.

How well named is the Boston suburb from an artistic standpoint? When Allston died in 1843, he was at the zenith of his reputation and was considered the foremost American artist of the day. He was especially highly regarded in Boston. When plans to establish the Boston Museum of Fine Arts were being formulated in 1870, Allston's painting *Elijah in the Desert* was the very first work purchased for inclusion. It was even suggested by one important donor that the museum be named in his honor, "as the one great artist in America." There was dissent, certainly, coming from those who regarded Allston, with his European frame of reference, as irrelevant to America's efforts to establish a national artistic identity.

With the passage of time, this perception of Allston as an anachronism grew. By the early twentieth century his reputation had receded to the point that he was often ignored altogether or dismissed as a minor figure.

A new appreciation of the importance and uniqueness of Allston's work came in the 1940s, however, in response chiefly to the writings of E.P. Richardson of the Detroit Institute of Art, the painter's principal biographer. Slowly Allston's reputation revived. A landmark exhibit of Allston's work at the Museum of Fine Arts in 1979, on the two hundredth anniversary of his birth, entitled "A Man of Genius" signaled Allston's full rehabilitation. The catalog of that exhibit described the namesake of our Allston district as "a sensitive portraitist, the first major American landscape painter, perhaps the country's most important historical painter, and the most versatile draftsman of his time."

13

JAMES HOLTON'S LEGACY
Founding the Brighton Public Library

Brighton was one of the earliest towns near Boston to establish a public library. The date of its establishment was 1864. The town took this important step when a local benefactor, James Holton, bequeathed it the substantial sum of $6,000 for the purchase of books for a public library. Had Holton not offered the town this sum, the Brighton Public Library, known as the Holton Library, might never have been established.

The movement for a public library (Brighton had been served by subscription libraries as early as 1827) was initiated in 1853, when a group of prominent citizens petitioned the Massachusetts legislature for the incorporation of a library association to be called the Union Association. According to its act of incorporation, this organization was established to provide "a lyceum, a public library, and courses of lectures on scientific and literary subjects." A lyceum is an organization that presents lectures, debates and dramatic performances. Lyceum lectures were very popular in the pre–Civil War period.

Unfortunately, the Union Association never materialized, presumably for lack of sufficient financial support. What the 1853 initiative demonstrates, however, is the existence in Brighton at an early date of a desire to establish a free public library. The projectors of the Union Association, it should be noted, included several of the town's most influential citizens; Nathaniel Martin and William R. Champney, two of Brighton's three selectmen, were incorporators, as were Edward C. Sparhawk, John Warren Hollis and Jacob F. Taylor, three of the town's wealthiest residents.

The establishment of the Brighton Library Association in 1858 marked the first concrete step toward the creation of a public library. That the goal of the incorporators of this private library association was the eventual creation of a public library is clear from Article V of its bylaws, which stipulated that "the trustees shall deliver up to the Town of Brighton, or persons authorized by the town to receive it, the library and other property of the association, whenever said Town of Brighton shall make suitable provision for the maintenance and increase of the library."

James Holton's Legacy

The Library Association made its home in the Brighton Town Hall in Brighton Center, another indication that it was intended for eventual conversion to a public library. At its inception, the Library Association possessed only about 1,300 books, a collection with a somewhat narrow compass. Notably, its trustees were slow to recognize native genius, for the library's shelves contained nothing by Whittier, Whitman or Parkman, and only a single volume apiece by Longfellow and Melville, the leading contemporary American authors.

It was James Holton's $6,000 bequest that finally motivated the town to establish a public library. The terms of the Holton will were very precise. The $6,000 sum was earmarked for the purchase of books, and books only. For the town to qualify to receive the money it had to provide "a suitable room and furniture, and appoint a suitable person and librarian, who shall safely keep said books and care for the same." Holton's will went on to provide that "if said town shall refuse to accept the bequest on the above-named terms, then I shall give and bequeath said six thousand dollars to my residuary legatees hereinafter named."

On April 8, 1864, the electors of Brighton, assembled in a town meeting, voted to accept the terms of James Holton's bequest and also to incorporate the collection of the Brighton Library Association into the new public facility, as provided for in that organization's bylaws.

Born in Brighton in 1800, James Holton was the eldest child of Major Benjamin Holton and Mary (Shed) Holton. When James was five, the family moved to the Deacon Hill house on Faneuil Street (on the site of the present Faneuil housing project). This was to be Holton's residence for the balance of his life. Holton never married. His wealth came from a combination of inheritance and personal success in maritime ventures. In his youth he frequently went to sea. Holton was also a deeply religious man who often traveled to Boston on Sundays to worship at the Seamen's Bethel in the North End. According to Reverend Frederic A. Whitney of the First Church (Unitarian), Holton "was deeply interested in modern spiritualism."

Reverend Whitney left a lengthy description of Holton. This portrait is rather unusual, however, in the degree to which it criticized this major public benefactor (a man who left a total of $60,000 to various public and private charities). "He always loved especially to help the deserving poor and needy," Whitney conceded, but "he would refuse aid to many really worthy causes not of his class, and thus, in the estimation of some, damage his generosity."

Opposite: James Holton, the Brighton philanthropist, who left the sum of $6,000 to the town for the purchase of books for a public library. Holton's bequest prompted the town fathers to establish a public library in 1864. *Courtesy of the Boston Public Library.*

One such element "not of his class" were Brighton's non-Protestant poor—the town's immigrant Irish, who were Roman Catholics, and who by 1860 comprised about one-third of the town's population and a disproportionately high percentage of those in need of charity. The will that contributed $6,000 for the creation of a local public library, left a like sum for the establishment of a Protestant Pauper Fund—in effect, thereby saying, "No Catholics need apply!" Clearly Holton harbored strong nativist sentiments. Yet, Whitney also noted, "Beneath [Holton's] almost repulsive plainness of exterior was a heart that beat for the welfare of his fellow creatures and, we believe, was right in God."

In 1873 the Town of Brighton built a handsome Gothic Revival–style building to house its fast-growing public library, naming it the Holton Library in honor of the benefactor James Holton. This was the last public building constructed by the town before its 1874 annexation to Boston. Sadly, the Holton Library was razed in the late 1960s to make way for the existing Brighton Branch library building. *Courtesy of the Boston Public Library.*

James Holton's Legacy

Once it had authorized the establishment of a public library, the April 8, 1864 Brighton town meeting proceeded to choose a board of trustees for the Brighton Public Library. John Ruggles, the headmaster of Brighton High School (the school was then situated on Academy Hill Road), was elected president of the board. Ruggles was a Harvard graduate. The posts of librarian and secretary went to J.P.C. Winship, son of the founder of Brighton's horticultural industry, later to become the historian of Brighton. Winship bore the responsibility for organizing the collection. Life Baldwin, president of the Market National Bank, served as treasurer. Other trustees included Reverend Whitney; Town Clerk William Wirt Warren; State Senator Joseph A. Pond; lumber dealer and master carpenter Granville Fuller (builder of the Brighton Town Hall); slaughterhouse proprietor Nathaniel Jackson; and Selectman Weare D. Bickford.

During its first ten years the Brighton Public Library was located on the first-floor, right-hand side of the Brighton Town Hall. The cost of outfitting these rooms came to $1,133,42.

The new public library opened its doors for the first time on September 1, 1864, in the midst of the Civil War (on the very day that the people of Brighton were examining the new facility, the city of Atlanta, Georgia, was being consumed by flames). John Ruggles made reference to the war in his first annual report of January 30, 1865: "We cannot forget," he intoned, "those of our number, who have not for months, and many of them for years, enjoyed the privileges and comforts of home. [But] even now," he wrote with obvious feelings of bitterness, "the sun is breaking through the noxious vapors and unwholesome exhalations which have been wafted hither from regions where free schools and free libraries are unknown."

Judging from its annual reports, the Brighton Public Library was from the outset extremely well patronized. Its collection grew very rapidly. By 1869, Brighton ranked fifth among Massachusetts towns in the size of its public library. By 1873, on the eve of annexation, the collection comprised an impressive eleven thousand volumes and had long since outgrown its Town Hall accommodations. The trustees began agitating for improved facilities as early as 1868. "The edifice used for a public library, its report of that year noted, should be devoted to that purpose alone, and this alike on grounds of freedom from noise and other interruptions and from exposure to fire."

The Town of Brighton approved construction of a separate library building in 1872. The Holton Library, a Victorian Gothic–style structure costing $70,000 and designed by Brighton-born architect George Fuller (son of lumber dealer Granville Fuller) stood on the site presently occupied by the Brighton Branch Library. This architecturally distinguished structure was nearing completion at the time of Brighton's annexation to Boston in January 1874.

14

COMMUTING IN EARLY
NINETEENTH-CENTURY BRIGHTON

Before 1816 no regularly scheduled transportation of any kind existed between Boston and its western suburbs. The first hourly stagecoach service to the outlying towns was established in 1826. By 1827 two stage lines connected Brookline and Brighton to the metropolis, one running through Brookline Village, the other across the Mill Dam and along the Brighton Road (lower Commonwealth and Brighton Avenues).

Prior to 1830 the Brookline–Brighton Center stagecoach stopped at the Bull's Head Tavern, the original home of the Brighton Cattle Market, located a quarter mile east of Brighton Center. However, with the construction of the Cattle Fair Hotel in Brighton Center in 1830, the stagecoach began stopping there.

A far more important form of public transportation was introduced in 1834, with the construction of the Boston and Worcester Railroad through Brighton. Though the building of a western railroad ultimately reinforced Brighton's position as the center of the cattle and slaughtering industries, support for the project was far from unanimous. Railroads brought hazards and inconveniences to the communities they crossed: noise, smoke, frightened horses, engines crossing streets at grade and the possibility of property damage from fires.

In addition, Brighton's economy was still largely tied to agriculture, farmers comprising nearly two-thirds of the town's workforce in 1830. The prosperity of Brighton's farms rested upon its proximity to the largest urban market in New England. If a western railroad were built, remote regions of the state would begin sending cheap produce to the city to compete with goods produced in Brighton. Thus the town's farmers had much to lose.

Commuting in Early Nineteenth-Century Brighton

Brighton Station.

2

The Brighton Depot, dating from 1834, situated in Winships' Gardens in north Brighton, was the first depot on the Boston and Worcester Railroad outside of Boston. Brighton residents could board the trains at this attractive North Brighton location and be in the heart of the city in twenty minutes. *Courtesy of the Brighton-Allston Historical Society Archives.*

Moreover, the Brighton cattle and slaughtering industry had no pressing need of the services that a railroad would provide. The herding of cattle over hundreds of miles from interior areas by farmers and drovers had been going on for decades. These overland cattle drives continued to be an important source of supply for the Brighton cattle market long after the construction of a western railroad.

There is no mention of the railroad issue in the Brighton town records of the late 1820s and early 1830s. This silence is rather surprising, given the town's propensity for taking strong positions on transportation issues. What appears to have happened (the evidence being admittedly circumstantial) is that a small group of political entrepreneurs, led by former State Senator Gorham Parsons, reached an understanding with the railroad whereby the town would raise no formal objection to the construction of the line, in exchange for moving it to the northern edge of town, a measure that would both safeguard property values in the more desirable and elevated sections of the community, as well as locate the railroad in an area where Brighton's principal officeholders held substantial acreage.

Significantly, the major officeholders in Brighton from 1830 to 1834 were chiefly North Brighton landowners. They included Francis Winship, part-owner of Winships' Gardens, who represented Brighton in the Massachusetts House of Representatives from 1823 to 1829 and in the Massachusetts State Senate from 1829 to 1833. Francis Winship also served on the Board of Selectmen from 1829 to 1832 and frequently presided over Brighton town meetings. The Brighton Depot was to be placed in Winships' Gardens, which worked to the advantage of the nursery since many of its patrons were Bostonians. From 1831 to 1835, these North Brighton men controlled the town's Board of Selectmen. Between 1833 and 1835, major North Brighton landowners held all three selectmen's seats. They were Edmund Rice, Dana Dowse and Cephas Brackett.

The rerouting of the Boston and Worcester Railroad from the center of the community to the northernmost part of town was extremely significant for the future of Brighton. If a railroad had been built through the Brighton Center area, as was originally proposed, nuisance industries would almost certainly have been more widely scattered over the face of the town. By confining the railroad to Brighton's northernmost section, Parsons and the other "solid men of Brighton" helped to foster a degree of industrial concentration.

Construction of the Boston and Worcester Railroad began in 1832. By the spring of 1834—with the line completed only as far as West Newton— service was inaugurated. In her reminiscences of early nineteenth-century Brighton, Mary Jane Kingsley Merwin wrote of this inaugural trip: "I was on the bridge in Winship's Gardens, and saw the first locomotive that passed over the road with passengers. It had a single car containing the officers who were making a trial trip as far as the road was finished, to West Newton, I think."

The establishment of Brighton's railroad depot at the center of Winships' Gardens helped to stimulate the development of North Brighton. By 1850 the area near to the depot, then known as Brighton Corners, had become the town's second largest commercial center, containing some fifteen business establishments, including two general stores, a hotel, a livery stable and two lumber yards. This neighborhood's share of the town's population, which had stood at a mere 6.4 percent in 1820, rose to almost 25 percent by 1850.

In addition, a substantial concentration of slaughterhouses, ropewalks and lumberyards soon lined the entire railroad corridor, giving the northern quarter of the town a distinctly industrial character.

The Boston and Worcester Railroad (B&W) also reinforced the position of the local cattle and slaughtering industries by offering special freight rates to anyone transporting cattle to the Brighton Stockyards. By 1850 Brighton was doing some $10 million a year of business in cattle and slaughtering, with much of the livestock now arriving by rail. The Brighton Depot at the foot of Market Street was actually making more money for the B&W than the line's elaborate downtown passenger depot at Lincoln and Beach Streets.

Commuting in Early Nineteenth-Century Brighton

Another mode of transportation came to Brighton in the 1830s: the omnibus, a horse-drawn wheeled conveyance (a kind of urban stagecoach), which moved along a set route on a regular schedule, carrying about a dozen passengers.

In 1839 Sumner Wellman, a local resident, established the first omnibus line in Brighton, which ran between Brighton Center and Boston by way of Brookline Village and Roxbury. The omnibus enjoyed important advantages over the railroad. Very little capital was needed to establish such a line, and the route could be altered at any time to take account of new development. Wellman was a man of relatively modest means. He owned no property whatsoever, apart from his horse-drawn vehicle. He drove the omnibus himself, alternating trips with his one employee, Daniel Hyde.

This line survived for twenty-one years. A major advantage for Wellman lay in an absence of competition on the Washington Street route. By 1845 his omnibus was making six trips a day, at 9:00 and 11:00 a.m. and at 1:00, 3:00, 6:00 and 9:00 p.m., for a fare of 25 cents (18½ cents from Brookline) each way, with tickets available in lots of six for a dollar (at an average cost of 16⅔ cents apiece). Eventually Wellman's line became what was termed an "hourly."

However, the lure of the omnibus was severely limited even for those who could afford to pay its relatively high fare, for these heavy horse-drawn vehicles were slow (averaging less than five miles an hour), uncomfortable and poorly ventilated. Not until the late 1850s was a more efficient mode of public transportation introduced—the horse-drawn streetcar.

15

The Coming of the Irish
to Brighton

The appearance of a recent article about contemporary Irish immigration
into Allston-Brighton got me thinking about the first great wave of
Irish immigrants that flooded into Brighton in the mid-nineteenth century
and the transforming impact that their arrival had upon the town's social,
economic and political life.

The Irish came to this country in huge numbers as a result of the Great
Famine. The potato rot, a disease that destroyed the most important source
of food for the Irish peasantry, first appeared in 1845, subjecting the
ordinary people of that benighted land to a succession of miseries that has
few parallels in modern history.

Ireland was a land of great estates, owned mostly by Protestant landlords.
With the failure of the potato crop, Irish cottagers were unable to pay their
rents and were accordingly driven from their holdings. The suffering of the
Irish people was particularly severe between 1849 and 1851, when some
one million were displaced. They emigrated, when they could, to England,
Canada and the United States. The flow slowed somewhat by the late
1850s, only to revive in the early 1860s, following the reappearance of the
dreaded potato rot. By 1865 some two and a half million Irish had fled their
homeland, many of them coming to New England.

The impact of this influx of Irish immigrants upon Brighton, a town of
about two thousand residents, was enormous. In the first ten years of the
phenomenon (between 1846 and 1855) the Irish Catholic population of
the town rose from a mere one hundred to more than one thousand—or
from about 5 percent to nearly 40 percent. In subsequent decades the

The coming of large numbers of Irish immigrants to Brighton in the post 1846 period led to the foundation in 1853 of the town's first Roman Catholic church, St. Columba's, located on Bennett Street. When the size of the congregation outstripped the modest wooden Bennett Street church in 1872, construction of the much larger St. Columbkille's church began around the corner on Market Street. *Courtesy of the Brighton-Allston Historical Society Archives.*

number continued rising until the Irish comprised a majority of Brighton's population.

Brighton, it should be emphasized, was not unique in this respect. Boston and most nearby towns experienced a substantial influx of immigrant Irish from 1846 to 1870. Generally speaking, the more commercially oriented a community, the more job-hungry Irish it attracted.

Not only were the Irish an extremely large group, but they were also almost all Roman Catholics—members of a church that Protestants looked upon with deep suspicion. The Irish were also a relatively young group. Less than 2 percent of them were over fifty years old, while nearly 80 percent were under thirty. Also, almost half of the adult Irish were unmarried.

Most importantly, the great majority had no marketable skills. In 1855, 60 percent of Brighton's Irish listed their occupation as "laborer" or "servant."

There were some skilled Irish in the town to be sure—seven blacksmiths, three butchers, three shoemakers, three gardeners, two stonemasons, two rope makers and two farmers—but the great majority of these immigrants had no skill for which a demand existed. That so few turned to farming may seem surprising, since most of the land surface of Brighton was then devoted to agriculture, but land was extremely expensive and the wages paid farm laborers were among the lowest of the low.

Many Irish took jobs in domestic service. Some 30 percent of Irish workers in Brighton in 1855 were employed in the households of the town's well-to-do residents, as maids, servants, gardeners and caretakers. This workforce consisted mostly of women.

Job opportunities for the unskilled were relatively plentiful during the boom period of the late 1840s and early 1850s. Irish laborers were needed to build new streets, sewerage, lighting and transit systems, and residential, commercial and public structures. And, while wages were low, working conditions often dangerous and work days long, a frugal immigrant might, with a bit of luck, succeed in accumulating enough savings to buy a house, or perhaps even go into business for himself.

Where did Brighton's Irish population reside in the early years? The largest concentration settled in North Brighton. Nearly half the total number of Irish families in the town in 1855 lived there, in the area north of the railroad tracks between Market and Franklin Streets, where the town's industrial facilities were largely concentrated. Another sizeable population lived on the south side of Brighton Center, principally along Winship, Shepard and Eastburn Streets. The first Catholic Mass in Brighton was celebrated in the mid-1840s in the home of Irish immigrant Thomas Corcoran on Eastburn Street. Another somewhat smaller concentration was to be found near Union Square. There were also many smaller clusters, usually situated adjacent to industrial and commercial establishments.

And what of the reaction of Brighton's native-born element to these newcomers? The Yankees (i.e., Anglo-Saxon Protestants) feared and distrusted the Irish. These animosities were deeply rooted in Anglo-Irish history. David Nevins, a wealthy Yankee manufacturer who owned an estate that comprised the present St. Gabriel's Monastery and St. Elizabeth's Hospital grounds, was so anti-Irish in attitude that he steadfastly refused to employ Irish servants or laborers. At one point, when the roof of his handsome mansion sprung a leak and he was unable to find a Yankee workman to repair it, he allowed the rain to pour in rather than employ an Irishman to make the necessary repairs.

Brighton's Protestants, it should be emphasized, were not unique in harboring strong anti-Irish sentiments. The political wing of the anti-immigrant and anti-Catholic or nativist movement—the so-called American or Know-Nothing Party—was extremely powerful in Massachusetts in the 1850s. In November 1854, the Know-Nothings not only won control of the Massachusetts State Legislature, but also managed to elect one of their own as governor, a Boston dry goods merchant named Henry Gardner. Gardner, in fact, served three consecutive terms as Massachusetts chief executive. The avowed object of the Know-Nothings was to deny voting and office-holding privileges to the foreign-born. Brighton, it should be noted, gave Henry Gardner 60 percent of its votes in the 1854 election. Gardner also topped the ticket here in the 1855 and 1856 elections.

One of the most important early consequences of the coming of the Irish to Brighton was the establishment of a Catholic church here, St. Columba's (later renamed St. Columbkille's), founded in 1855. The church was originally situated near the northeast corner of Bennett and Market Streets.

By 1872 St. Columbkille's had outgrown its original wooden building, and began constructing a much larger stone edifice at the corner of Market and Arlington Streets, which was completed in 1880.

Another important consequence of the coming of the Irish was a gradual shift in the town's political orientation toward the Democratic Party, which had been founded in the late 1820s by the followers of Andrew Jackson, but had never received much support here. As late as the 1848 to 1852 period, the opposing Whigs commanded between 61 and 67 percent of Brighton's vote. By the end of the 1850s, however, the Democrats, who made a point of recruiting immigrant support, moved into a position of parity with the competition, the recently formed Republican Party. By the 1870s, Brighton was a Democratic stronghold, the only town in Middlesex County to regularly vote Democratic.

Politics was one of the avenues by which the most talented Irish immigrants and their sons achieved prominence in the early years. Significantly on the eve of Brighton's 1874 annexation to Boston, several of the town's most important officeholders were Irish—Patrick Moley sat on the three-member Board of Selectmen and Harvard-educated attorney Michael Norton held the posts both of town clerk and town treasurer.

Equally significant were the successes of Irish businessmen in the early years, especially in the livestock and slaughtering trades, in hotel and saloon keeping, and as small-scale manufacturers. In the fullness of time, the Town of Brighton (present-day Allston-Brighton) turned out to be a rather good choice for the victims of Ireland's Great Famine.

16

THOMAS W. SILLOWAY
Allston's Master Builder

Thomas W. Silloway, a resident of Union Square, Allston, may well hold the record as the architect of the greatest number of churches in the country. When he died at his 15 North Beacon Street home on May 17, 1910, at age eighty-one, the *Boston Transcript* credited him with having designed over four hundred religious edifices all over the eastern part of the United States, from Maine to South Carolina to Minnesota.

But Silloway's output wasn't limited to churches. This incredibly prolific architect also designed schools, academies, colleges, libraries, asylums, town halls and many private residences during a career that spanned some sixty years. His best-known structure is a landmark government building: the handsome State Capitol in Montpelier, Vermont. Other buildings by Silloway of note included the Goddard Seminary in Barre, Vermont, and Butchel College in Akron, Ohio.

What makes Silloway's architectural output especially surprising is the dual career he pursued, for in addition to designing buildings, he was a Universalist preacher. It was in the capacity of a minister that he first appeared on the Brighton scene in 1863, as pastor of the Universalist Church at 541 Cambridge Street (the building that would later house the Brighthelmstone Club and now accommodates Helping Hands). Silloway designed this edifice in 1861.

Thomas William Silloway was born in Newburyport, Massachusetts, on August 7, 1828, the eldest son of Thomas Silloway Sr., a coppersmith who maintained a business on Elbow Lane, and of Susan (Stone) Silloway. He was educated in the public schools of his birthplace, at Brown High and the local Latin School.

Thomas W. Silloway

Thomas Silloway, minister and architect of Brighton's Universalist Church, over which he officiated from 1863 to 1867. Silloway is credited with having designed some four hundred churches in the northeastern United States in the course of a long and distinguished career. *Courtesy of the Brighton-Allston Historical Society Archives.*

Silloway's youth was marked by much indecisiveness. As a young boy, he worked as a clerk in a West India goods store. Then in 1845, at age sixteen, his father apprenticed him to Robert Gunnison, a housewright, to learn the trade of carpentry. Silloway was probably unhappy with Gunnison, for he soon abandoned this apprenticeship and opened a West India Dry Goods store of his own, but this too proved a temporary situation. In a day when young men were expected to make an early commitment to a trade or occupation, this indecisiveness must have generated a certain amount of family tension.

An additional source of tension stemmed from young Silloway's 1844 decision to abandon the religion in which his parents had raised him (Methodism) for Universalism, a creed that rejected the doctrine of original sin and held that all men were destined for salvation. Not only did Silloway reject his parents' Methodist faith, but he also "ardently engaged in the promulgation of the doctrines of [Universalism]."

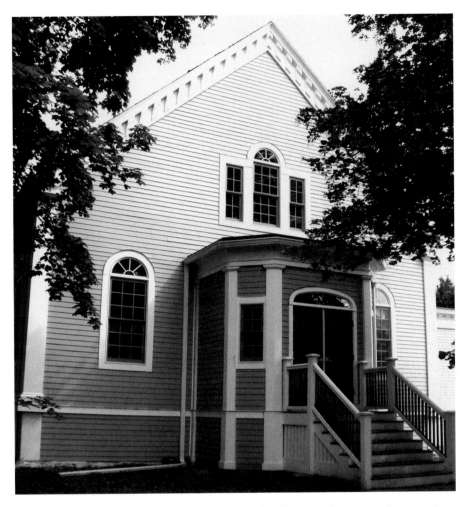

Above: The Universalist church experienced much alteration over the years and as recently as the 1990s was sheathed in vinyl siding with its Italianate detailing completely hidden from view. Its current owner, Helping Hands, recently restored this handsome local landmark to an appearance suggestive of its earlier incarnation. *Photo by William P. Marchione.*

Opposite: Silloway not only served as the minister of Brighton's Universalist Church, but also designed the handsome Italianate-style building, which still stands on Cambridge Street in Allston. Here we see the structure as it appeared about 1900 when it was the headquarters of the Brighthelmstone Club, the local branch of the American Federation of Women's Clubs. *Courtesy of the Brighton-Allston Historical Society Archives.*

In 1847 at age twenty, Silloway left his parents' home and moved to Boston to study architecture under Ammi B. Young, the man who in 1838 had designed Boston's handsome Customs House. Here he finally found his niche. Pursuing a full course under Young's capable tutelage, in 1851 Silloway began practicing architecture on his own account in Boston.

Silloway was a highly successful architect from the start. His earliest commissions included two important structures in Milford, Massachusetts, the Pearl Street Universalist Church and a handsome new Greek Revival Town Hall, both completed in 1851–52. A contemporary writer described the latter structure as "built in the pure Roman style," large enough to accommodate eleven hundred people standing and costing a substantial $20,000.

In 1857, when he was only twenty-nine years old, Silloway received the most important commission of his career. He was hired to design a new capitol building for the state of Vermont. The original 1836 Vermont State House, the work of his mentor Ammi B. Young, had been gutted by fire in January 1857. Since Young was then serving as the principal architect of the Capitol in Washington, D.C., he was unavailable to supervise the Vermont project, and presumably recommended his former pupil for the assignment.

Silloway did an extraordinary job in Montpelier. The great architect Stanford White later described the 1858 Vermont capitol as the finest example of Greek Revival architecture in the country. But to the manifest annoyance of those charged with overseeing the project's finances, Silloway insisted that only the very best (and most expensive) materials be used in his building. This emphasis on quality resulted in his being fired from the supervising architect's post just as the project was brought to conclusion. In 1862, however, perhaps by way of compensation, the University of Vermont conferred an honorary MA on the young man in recognition of his significant contributions to the architecture of that state.

That same year Silloway entered upon his second career, that of a Universalist minister. Over the next five years he served churches in Kingston, New Hampshire, in Boston's North End (the First Universalist Church of Boston at the corner of Hanover and North Bennett Streets) and, finally, the Brighton church, over which he officiated from 1863 to 1867, relinquishing the post only when the increasing number of architectural commissions became so burdensome as to preclude his properly attending to his pastoral duties. In the last year of his Brighton pastorate, this master builder executed no fewer than twenty-five commissions, which included twelve new churches, seven remodeled churches, four residences and two schools. Another factor that may have prompted his retirement from the ministry was his bachelor status. Silloway never married, and a pastor without a wife is always at a distinct disadvantage.

After relinquishing his pulpit, the busy architect lived for a time at 71 Green Street in Boston's West End, in the same building where he maintained his architectural office.

But Allston-Brighton had not seen the last of its distinguished minister and architect. About 1870 Silloway moved back, and built the ornate Queen Anne–style house at 40 Gordon Street in Allston, now the community's only San Francisco–style "painted lady."

Silloway also involved himself in public affairs. In 1870 he spoke before a committee of the Massachusetts legislature urging adoption of the so-called Six Mile Bill, which would have incorporated Brighton, Brookline and West Roxbury into the City of Boston. As an architect and builder, he was distressed by the low quality of the public services that the Town of Brighton was then providing its residents, especially in the areas of street repair, sewerage and lighting, and believed that absorption by Boston would lead to improvements that would foster desirable residential development.

Silloway was also a man of broad interests, who published several books. His writings ranged from architecture to theology to sacred music to travel. One of his best-known works was *Cathedral Towns of England, Ireland, and Scotland*, which he wrote with Lee L. Powers. Silloway was also deeply interested in history. He was an active member of the New England Historical Genealogical Society from 1864 to the end of his life.

In the late 1870s, Silloway sold his Gordon Street residence and moved back to the West End. In 1886, when an earthquake did major damage to Charleston, South Carolina, he received another key commission—the job of supervising the reconstruction of six of that city's damaged churches. Then, in 1890, he moved back to Allston, to 15 North Beacon Street (a house that was demolished many years ago), where he resided during the final twenty years of his life.

For the benefit of readers who might wish to view some of the Silloway-designed structures in the Greater Boston area, I offer this additional list: the Church of the Unity at 91 West Newton Street in the South End (1859); the First Universalist Church in Arlington (1860); the Fourth Baptist Church in South Boston (1864); the Second Methodist Church in East Boston (1865); Dean Academy in Franklin (1867); the North Congregational Church in Newburyport (1867); the South Abington Congregationalist Church (1867); the Milton Congregationalist Church (1867); the Rockport Town Hall (1869); the Winthrop Street Methodist Church in Roxbury Highlands (1869); the Cambridge Soldier's Monument (1869); the North Congregationalist Church in Lynn (1869); the Pilgrim Congregationalist Church in Cambridgeport (1871); the Attleboro Town Hall (1871); the Medfield Town Hall (1872); the Wood Memorial Church in Cambridge (1883); and the Zion Evangelical Lutheran Church in the South End.

17

BUILDING THE CHESTNUT HILL RESERVOIR

In 1880 S.F. Smith, a Newton historian, described the Chestnut Hill Reservoir on the Brighton-Newton boundary, in the following glowing terms:

> *The spot is a lovely one. There are cultivated hills around the basin from which fine views may be had of its winding and graceful lines, and its sparkling sheets of water...The scenery is pleasantly diversified with glimpses of deep blue water, and groves of trees and plots of green grass.*

Smith went on to proclaim the reservoir a "perpetual benediction" to the area. He also expressed the hope that Boston's public park system would eventually be extended to include it, noting that the "Chestnut Hill Park [would] be a fitting culmination of a landscape beautiful and tasteful in nature and art."

Smith's observations reflect the key role the Chestnut Hill Reservoir played in the early history of Boston's developing park system. The reservoir was, of course, intended primarily as a water supply facility, but from its inception it also served as an important recreational resource for the people of Boston.

The Chestnut Hill Reservoir was constructed between 1866 and 1870. Since 1848 Boston's water supply had been conveyed to the city from Lake Cochituate in Framingham via an aqueduct passing through Newton Lower Falls, Waban and Newton Center to four small reservoirs near the city, located in Brookline, on Beacon Hill and in South and East Boston.

The Chestnut Hill Reservoir Gateway was erected in 1870 at the intersection of Chestnut Hill Avenue and the entrance of the Chestnut Hill Reservoir Driveway. It stood until 1895 when the extension of Commonwealth Avenue into Newton was constructed, necessitating its removal. *Courtesy of the Brighton-Allston Historical Society Archives.*

In 1859 a major break occurred in the aqueduct at the point where it passed across the Charles River at the westerly end of Needham. Since the capacity of the four small storage reservoirs ringing the city was quite limited, it became necessary to shut off water service to Boston for all but domestic uses while repairs were being made. Had a major fire broken out at this point, the fast-growing metropolis might have found itself without water, with devastating consequences. This emergency prompted the Cochituate Water Board to recommend the construction of a much larger storage reservoir just outside of Boston.

It was five years, however, before the first definite steps were taken to provide the new reservoir, a delay the water board blamed on the poor economic climate of the Civil War years. In 1864 the Boston city engineer recommended a site on the Brighton-Newton boundary for the facility, and in April 1865, Governor John Andrew signed a bill authorizing the water board to "take and hold, by purchase or otherwise" up to two hundred acres of land near Chestnut Hill bordered by South Street on the north (now Commonwealth Avenue), Beacon Street on the south, Chestnut Hill Avenue on the east and an unnamed street "leading from said South Street to said Beacon Street on the west." Brighton's Evergreen Cemetery, which had been laid out in 1851, was explicitly excluded from the tract.

In all 212½ acres were purchased by the water board from eighteen local landowners. The largest single parcel, fifty-eight acres, came from the estate of Amos Adams Lawrence, the great textile manufacturer, whose mansion stood on the heights where the Boston College complex was later constructed. Other large purchases, totaling eighty acres, came from the Monroe, Wilson and Warren families of Brighton.

During 1865 the various land purchases were completed, surveys were made and trees and brush were cleared from the location. Formal construction of the reservoir did not begin, however, until the spring of 1866. Henry M. Wightman, who had conducted the surveys, was appointed resident engineer to oversee construction on a day-to-day basis.

The first work done by teams of horses began in April 1866. The contract for teams went to two Brighton men, Benjamin F. Ricker and George A. Wilson. Ricker owned the largest livery stable in Boston, located on School Street. By October 1868, this firm had eighty-eight teams at work on the site. The sum expended on teaming, $474,000, represented more than 20 percent of the total cost of the project.

The Chestnut Hill Reservoir was a major public works endeavor, the largest waterworks project in the history of the city. The plan called for two storage basins, separated by a watertight dam. The smaller of these bodies of water, the Lawrence Basin (which was filled by Boston College in the 1950s) covered 37½ acres, while the larger Bradlee Basin (the surviving reservoir) covered 87½ acres.

The building of a formal driveway around the reservoir, designed exclusively for recreational use, was proposed during the summer of 1866, an idea that won immediate and enthusiastic public support. After considerable debate, the water board directed its engineer to prepare a plan for an eighty-foot-wide roadway. Beginning at a great entrance arch, this roadway extended around the northern and western sides of the facility, joining Beacon Street to complete its circuit of the reservoir. At the entrance gate this roadway was some thirty feet above the surface of the water, then fell gradually until, at its intersection with Beacon Street, it was only slightly higher than the reservoir basins.

While no single individual is credited with having been the architect of the reservoir, the most important design influence was probably Nathaniel J. Bradlee, who served either as a member or as president of the water board throughout the period of construction. One of the leading Boston architects of his day, Bradlee designed over five hundred Boston buildings. The naming of the larger of the two Chestnut Hill Reservoir basins in his memory is indicative of the key role he played, as was his subsequent authorship of the first published history of the reservoir.

The building of the reservoir was not without its mishaps. In March 1867, the entire workforce struck for higher wages. The water board, which was intent upon keeping costs to a minimum, immediately fired and replaced

The Chestnut Hill Reservoir Driveway was a favorite place of resort for Bostonians owning private horse-drawn conveyances. Only six miles from downtown, its driveway provided one of the most scenic and varied locations west of the city. *Courtesy of the Brighton-Allston Historical Society Archives.*

these strikers. The daily wage at the reservoir in 1867 was $1.50 and the average workday was twelve to fourteen hours, depending on daylight, but in this era of an abundant labor supply, workers had little bargaining power. The bulk of the reservoir workforce consisted of Canadian maritime and Irish immigrant laborers. Temporary shelters were constructed on site to accommodate this horde of workmen, who numbered close to eight hundred at the height of the project.

In 1868 work was concentrated as much as possible on the smaller Lawrence Basin on the western end of the reservoir. This basin was formally opened that fall by water board President Bradlee, who noted in his dedicatory remarks that more than 240,000 cubic yards of material had been removed from the site. The storage capacity of the Lawrence Basin was 180 million gallons.

The larger Bradlee Basin was completed in the fall of 1870. This magnificent body of water (the surviving basin), has a storage capacity of 550 million gallons and a circumference of 1.56 miles.

The magnitude of this great public works project—the largest undertaken to that date by the City of Boston—is conveyed by the following statistics: Of the 212 acres comprising the reservoir grounds, 125 were under water, leaving 87 acres for passive recreational uses. The total water storage capacity of the reservoir was 731 million gallons, enough water to supply Boston for forty days. A 2,000-foot artificial dam was constructed on the reservoir's eastern end, facing Beacon Street. It was 35 feet high, 25 feet wide at the top, and 150 feet at the widest part of its base. The reservoir was lined with 2½-foot-thick dry rubble masonry, capped with granite blocks. The sewer, which was built to carry off the drainage of the valley, was 7,980 feet in length. To build it required 1,367,000 bricks and 4,300 barrels of cement. For much of its length this giant sewer was 15 to 20 feet below the ground. The reservoir was furnished, initially, with three handsome stone gatehouses—the Influent, Intermediate and Effluent Gatehouses—that controlled the flow of water through the system.

On October 25, 1870, the twenty-second anniversary of the opening of the Cochituate Water Works, a delegation consisting of President Bradlee, Boston Mayor Nathaniel Shurtleff, members of the water board, the Boston Board of Aldermen and the Boston City Council, dedicated the completed Chestnut Hill Reservoir. In his remarks to the assembled guests, Bradlee noted that the cost of the project, $2.4 million, had exceeded expectations, but expressed confidence that all would recognize that "its value is in the security it gives to the life and health of the inhabitants" of the burgeoning City of Boston.

18

Using the Chestnut Hill Reservoir

At the time of the opening of the Chestnut Hill Reservoir in 1870, the City of Boston maintained only two other large parks, the Boston Common and the Boston Public Garden, both located in the heart of the city. The reservoir, by contrast, lay in distant Chestnut Hill, more than five miles west of City Hall, outside of the city's corporate limits. This changed in 1874, when Boston annexed Brighton (Newton simultaneously ceding its portion of the reservoir to the city). As late as 1883, all of Boston's other parks together (there were forty-six of them in all) comprised less than 130 acres, as compared to the Chestnut Hill Reservoir's 212½ acres. Thus for the first decade and a half after its opening, the Chestnut Hill Reservoir comprised 62 percent of the city's parkland.

Greatly enhancing the attractiveness of this unique pleasure ground—so much larger and topographically striking than parks downtown—were its handsome architectural elements, three Greek Revival–style stone gatehouses.

The Influent Gatehouse, which regulated the flow of water from its source at Lake Cochituate, was situated on the western rim of the smaller Lawrence Basin. This structure was, unfortunately, demolished in 1950 when Boston College expanded its campus onto the site.

The Intermediate Gatehouse, regulating the flow of water between the basins, stood on the western side of the central driveway. This structure still stands, though it is now situated on the Boston College campus.

The third of the original structures, the Effluent Gatehouse, controlled the flow of water from the reservoir to the various small feeder reservoirs closer to downtown. A handsome two-story structure, surmounted by a hip roof, it was the largest and most elaborately detailed of the original structures, lying on the rim of the dam that encloses the eastern side of the Bradlee Basin. The original approach to the Effluent Gatehouse was a formal tree-lined driveway, fronted by a handsome fountain.

The Boston Water Board expended much time, energy and money on maintaining and improving the Chestnut Hill Reservoir in the years that followed. The most casual reading of the Boston Water Board's annual reports makes this abundantly clear. The 1880 report, for example, noted that "the structures connected with the Chestnut-Hill Reservoir are all in good order...the grounds are showing finely the results of past labor...of planting small and inexpensive trees for future effect, the ground...being gradually improved on a year-by-year basis."

In the late 1880s it was proposed to make the reservoir the focal point of Boston's developing park system. Had this scheme been adopted, Brighton's Aberdeen neighborhood would have become a 160-acre public park, and along with the adjacent reservoir, would today comprise nearly 400 acres of publicly owned open space.

This handsome 1890 photo shows the approach from Beacon Street to Gatehouse Number 1, the largest of the three original Greek Revival–style structures that were built on the margin of the Chestnut Hill Reservoir. *Courtesy of the Brighton-Allston Historical Society Archives.*

Using the Chestnut Hill Reservoir

In any event, the Chestnut Hill Reservoir was from the beginning a highly valued recreational facility. Edward Stanwood, author of the popular guidebook *Boston Illustrated*, took note of this in the late 1870s:

> *A magnificent driveway, varying from sixty to eighty feet in width surrounds the entire work, and is one of the great attractions of the suburbs of Boston. It is, in fact, the most popular drive in the vicinity. In some parts the road runs along close to the embankment, separated from it only by the beautiful graveled walk with the sodding on either side. It leaves the embankment and rises to a higher level at a little distance, from which an uninterrupted view of the entire reservoir can be had. The scenery in the neighborhood is so varied that it would of itself make this region a delightful one for pleasure driving, without the added attractions of the charming sheet of water, the graceful curvatures of the road, and the neat, trim appearance of the greensward that lines it through its entire length.*

Among the many thousands who utilized the reservoir grounds in the late 1870s was a future president of the United States, Theodore Roosevelt, during his courtship of the beautiful Alice Hunnewell Lee of Chestnut Hill (the Lee Mansion stood less than six hundred yards south of the Bradlee Basin). The couple tied the marital knot in October 1880.

The facility continued to be extremely popular in the years that followed. The following description of the grounds appeared in 1916, almost fifty years after its opening:

> *All around the winding outlines of the basin runs a trim driveway, and besides [sic] it a smooth gravel footpath. On all sides of the lake are symmetrical knolls, covered with forest trees and the greenest of turf. The banks to the waters edge are sodded and bordered with flowered shrubs; and the stonework, which in one place carries the road across a natural chasm, and the great natural ledges, are mantled over with clinging vines, and in autumn are aflame with the crimson of the ampelopsis and the Virginia creeper.*

The Chestnut Hill Reservoir became a favorite place of resort for Bostonians of all classes—not only the wealthy families of adjacent Chestnut Hill and those Bostonians fortunate enough to own private carriages, but also the less privileged residents of adjacent towns. The archives of the Brighton-Allston Historical Society contain many photographs attesting to the use of the reservoir grounds by families of limited means.

A development of great importance, which helped make the Chestnut Hill Reservoir more accessible to the general public, was the construction of new roads linking Boston with the reservoir via Kenmore Square. In the late 1880s, Brookline's Beacon Street was transformed from a county road into a 160-foot wide Parisian-style boulevard—the most elegant roadway in the Boston suburbs. Then, in the early 1890s, another boulevard was built through adjacent Brighton: Commonwealth Avenue. These two thoroughfares, both serviced by streetcar lines (the Beacon Street line dating from 1889; the Commonwealth Avenue line from 1909) were joined at the foot of the reservoir by the intersecting portion of Chestnut Hill Avenue to form the so-called Chestnut Hill Loop. The designer of these roadways, so serviceable to those desiring to reach the reservoir grounds, was the great landscape architect Frederick Law Olmsted, who had earlier laid out New York's Central Park, and was even then creating Boston's splendid Emerald Necklace park system.

A number of new buildings had meanwhile been constructed at the Chestnut Hill Reservoir, further enhancing its attractiveness. Between 1872 and 1898, the Boston Water Board tapped the Sudbury River and its tributaries, thereby adding sixty-two square miles of additional watershed area and over nineteen billion gallons of storage capacity to Boston's water system. In 1878 the strikingly handsome Sudbury Gatehouse was built opposite the intersection of the Chestnut Hill Driveway and Beacon Street to handle this new supply. In the late nineteenth century construction was also begun on the giant Wachusett Dam, which drew upon the waters of the Ware River Valley.

This continuous expansion of the Boston waterworks system led to the construction, toward the end of the nineteenth century, of the most elaborate reservoir buildings—two giant pumping stations on Beacon Street opposite the Bradlee Basin. The High Service Pumping Station, a magnificent brownstone Richardsonian Romanesque–style building designed by Boston City Architect Arthur H. Vinal, was constructed in 1887–88, with a wing added in 1897 by the architectural firm of Wheelwright and Haven. In designating this building a city landmark in the late 1980s, the Boston Landmarks Commission took note of its "bold…use of granite and freestone in cathedral-like grandeur," and its highly successful integration of building and landscape on a parcel "well suited to Richardsonian massing and horizontality."

In 1890 a small, handsome stone carriage house was constructed just east of the High Service edifice.

The Low Service Pumping Station, on the eastern end of the complex, a Beaux Arts Classical–style building, dates from 1898 to 1900, and is the work of the distinguished architectural firm of Shepley, Rutan and Coolidge.

Using the Chestnut Hill Reservoir

These distinguished late nineteenth-century buildings, one source tells us, were to serve as "the main hub of the Boston water supply system for the next sixty years."

It was the growing importance of the Chestnut Hill Reservoir to Greater Boston's water supply system that prompted the Metropolitan District Commission to fence off the inner ring of pedestrian pathways from public access, the beginning of a long spiral of deterioration and neglect for the reservoir as a recreational facility. Fortunately, the grounds were recently reopened by the Massachusetts Department of Conservation and Recreation and efforts are underway to restore this exquisite site to its historic function as a recreational facility for the people of Greater Boston.

19

THE HOTELS OF
BRIGHTON CENTER

Late nineteenth-century Brighton was unique in its unusually large number of hotels—some twenty-two in all. This article will focus upon the seven hotels situated in Brighton Center near the Brighton Cattle Market.

The hundreds of livestock dealers who came to Brighton each week to trade at Brighton's Cattle Market needed overnight accommodations. The local hotel industry was essential to the smooth operation of the local cattle industry. Since the focal point of that trade, prior to 1884, was Brighton Center, no fewer than seven of these hotels were concentrated there.

The most famous and the largest of Brighton's hostelries was the Cattle Fair Hotel, which stood on the north side of Washington Street, between present-day Market and Leicester Streets. It was built in 1830 by the Cattle Fair Hotel Corporation.

In petitioning the state legislature for incorporation, the organizers explained that there were then only two inns in the central part of Brighton (the Bull's Head Tavern on Washington Street a quarter mile east of the village, and Hastings Tavern standing on the site where the Cattle Fair Hotel would afterward be built); that these hostelries could not accommodate "the great influx of travelers who with drovers, farmers and many others" visited the Brighton Cattle Market each week; that it was therefore essential that a "much more spacious and convenient accommodation" be provided; and that in addition to building a large hotel, the sponsors were prepared to furnish "extensive pens and enclosing yards…whereby part of the vast droves of cattle and sheep which are constantly coming in may be left with more security to wait the best chance for a market." The act of incorporation required that the Cattle Fair Hotel provide *a shed or sheds, not less than two hundred feet by eighteen on the ground, and suitable for the shelter of horses and carriages, and conveniently located for the use of the public, to whom it shall be free of all charge for use thereof, and good and convenient barns, with suitable and sufficient stalls to secure and feed not less than one hundred head of neat cattle.*

These structures accommodated the Brighton Stockyards, which were located to the rear of Cattle Fair Hotel from 1830 to 1884.

The Cattle Fair was the largest hotel in any town around Boston. A February 1834 advertisement described the establishment in these terms:

The accommodations of this house are upon the most extensive scale. It has been arranged with particular attention to the traveler and drover, both as to comfort and convenience. Cotillion parties, engine companies, clubs and all associations [are] provided for at instant notice. The larder will always be provided with the best the seasons afford, and the bar, as well as every other part of the house, will be attended to with strict reference to comfort, convenience, and satisfaction of the patrons of this establishment.

The Cattle Fair Hotel is seen here as it looked following its 1852 renovation by leading Boston architect William Washburn. The largest hotel on the outskirts of Boston, it contained one hundred rooms, a huge dance hall on its top floor and a dining room that could seat up to five hundred people at a single sitting. Until their removal in 1884, the Brighton Stockyards were located to the rear of this landmark hostelry. *Courtesy of the Brighton-Allston Historical Society Archives.*

The second largest hotel near Brighton Center was the popular Brighton Hotel, the converted Winship Mansion. Samuel Dudley bought the Winship Mansion in 1820, substantially enlarged the building and converted it to a hotel. The Marquis de Lafayette stayed here when he visited Brighton in the mid-1820s during his tour of the United States on the fiftieth anniversary of American independence. The Brighton Hotel was taken down in the early 1890s to make way for the present District 14 police station. *Courtesy of the Brighton-Allston Historical Society Archives.*

The first proprietor of the Cattle Fair Hotel was Judson Murdock. The manager in 1834 was Zachariah B. Porter, the hotel keeper for whom the porterhouse steak was named, and who afterward owned and managed a famous hostelry in Porter Square, Cambridge, from which that location derived its name.

The Cattle Fair Hotel accommodated many prominent visitors, including U.S. Senators Daniel Webster and Henry Clay. Webster frequently visited Brighton to attend the annual Brighton Fair and Cattle Show, held in October. Clay came to Brighton in 1833 and is said to have recognized some cattle of his own raising that had been driven to Brighton on foot from his Lexington, Kentucky plantation.

In 1852 the Cattle Fair Hotel was renovated and enlarged in the then popular Italianate style by prominent Boston architect William Washburn. Broad-running verandas and a fourth story were added, giving the hotel a capacity of one hundred rooms. The manager at the time was William

Wilson, who was described as "a very popular man" under whose management "the hotel became a noted summer resort, accommodating thousands yearly and enjoying the reputation of being the best hotel outside of Boston. It possessed at that time the largest bar room in America." Later in the century its name was changed to the Faneuil House.

With the removal of the stockyards to North Brighton in 1884, the amount of business at the Faneuil House declined sharply. It was demolished in the 1890s to allow for residential development of the former cattle yard acreage.

The Brighton Hotel, situated on the site now occupied by the Brighton police station, had once been the Winship Mansion (built in 1780), home of the founders of the Brighton Cattle Market. In 1820 Jonathan and Francis Winship sold the old mansion to Samuel Dudley who, adding a floor and an extension to the rear, converted the building to a hotel. It was here that the Marquis de Lafayette stayed while visiting the United States in 1825 on the fiftieth anniversary of the Revolution.

Sleighing parties set out in season from the front of the Brighton Hotel for a "brush" down Cambridge Street and Brighton Avenue (then known as the Brighton Road) to the Back Bay's Milldam. Called Wilson's Hotel in its last years, this popular inn closed its doors in 1875. It was demolished in the early 1890s to make way for the District 14 Police Station.

Across Washington Street, at the southwest corner of Winship Street (on the site of the present Winship Spa), stood the Nagle Hotel. Eugene Nagle operated a hotel here in the late 1860s. However, the original building was partially demolished in the early 1870s when the town widened Washington Street. A short time later a second Nagle hotel opened on the same site. By 1900 it was owned by the Fitzgerald family and had assumed the name of its owners. State restrictions on the sale of liquor and the death of John F. Fitzgerald, the last proprietor, led to the closing of Fitzgerald Hotel in 1892.

At the corner of Wirt and Washington Streets, on the site now occupied by the law offices of Edward Gottlieb, stood the Reservoir House, which was established in the late 1860s while the Chestnut Hill Reservoir was under construction. The building was not original to the site, having been moved from Beacon Street in Boston. The original proprietor, Thomas Mullen, was an Irish immigrant. In 1912 the hotel, then called the Court Hotel (owing to its proximity to the original site of the Brighton Municipal Court House in the Old Town Hall) closed and was moved to 60 Henshaw Street, where it still stands, thus clearing the way for the construction of the Brighton Five Cent Savings Bank. A Mr. Ward owned the hotel in its final days. The first floor had a bar and stools for customers and a background of stained glass windows.

On March 23, 1872, an unsigned article entitled "A Trip to Brighton" appeared in the *Brighton Messenger*, which described the three hotels at the eastern end of Brighton Center in these terms:

> *I arrived at last, somewhat fatigued, at the Brighton Hotel and partook of lunch, for which the establishment of Mr. [Josiah] Wilson has been celebrated. If ever a man knew how to "keep a hotel" he is the man. I sauntered out, and the first building to meet my gaze was Nagle's Hotel, lately much improved, and which in the skillful hands of Mr. and Mrs. Nagle, carries on a flourishing business, as does also the Reservoir House, nearly opposite.*

At the southeast corner of Chestnut Hill Avenue and Washington Street stood Scates Hotel, operated by Mr. Dodenah Scates. This structure, which still stands, is the oldest building in Brighton Center. Constructed in 1818, and located originally on the site of the Winship School at the top of Dighton Street, it originally served as the exhibition hall of the Massachusetts Society for Promoting Agriculture, called Agricultural Hall, and was the focal point of the annual Brighton Fair and Cattle Show, held on Agricultural Hill from 1819 to the late 1830s. In the 1840s, the building was moved off the hill to the Chestnut Hill Avenue location and converted into Scates Hotel.

The last of Brighton Center's hotels, the Rockland House opened in the late 1870s and stood at the southeast corner of Washington Street and Academy Hill Road (then called Rockland Street). The building now houses Porter Bellys Bar and Grille. The original proprietor, John H. Lee, became a prominent political figure in the 1890s, representing Brighton on the Boston Board of Aldermen.

In a day when the temperance and prohibition movements enjoyed wide support, Brighton had a reputation as a wide-open town. Even when state law forbade its sale, alcohol could usually be obtained at Brighton's many hotels and saloons. The *Brighton Messenger*, published from 1872 to 1876, documents this illegal commerce with many references to State Constable Hoyt raiding local establishments, seizing liquor supplies and imposing stiff fines on Brighton's guilty hotel and saloonkeepers. Gamblers also found it easy to indulge their habit in Brighton.

A *Brighton Messenger* correspondent, writing on November 2, 1872, a year before Brighton's annexation to Boston, commented as follows about the effect these drinking establishments had upon Brighton's somewhat unsavory reputation, a complaint that has a distinctly modern ring to it:

The Hotels of Brighton Center

Brighton, I believe, is considered the refuge of all that is bad, and the den of vice. Go where you may, and a slur is cast upon her fair name. Now it is not Brighton or her towns-people that are so much worse, but it is the people who come into the village, and think when they get here it is no matter, only Brighton, we can do just as we please.

20

ANNEXATION SPURNED
Brookline's 1873 Rejection of Boston

On October 7, 1873, the neighboring towns of Brookline, Brighton and West Roxbury faced a momentous decision—whether to continue to be self-governing entities or to relinquish their political independence to the City of Boston.

The answers the voters of these three towns gave to that question were strikingly different. While Brighton and West Roxbury endorsed annexation by large majorities, more than two-thirds of Brookline's voters emphatically rejected the opportunity to join Boston.

This 1873 rejection of annexation by Brookline marked a decisive turning point in Boston's territorial growth. Between 1868 and 1873, five communities—Roxbury, Dorchester, Charlestown, Brighton and West Roxbury—opted to merge with the city, thereby increasing Boston's area fivefold and adding some 108,000 new residents to its population. Brookline's rejection of annexation took the wind out of a seemingly irresistible consolidation movement. Boston would, in fact, absorb no more towns for nearly forty years, until 1912, when Hyde Park became the last suburb to approve a merger.

What prompted Brookline to make this historic and precedent-setting 1873 decision? Of all the towns on the edge of Boston, Brookline was the most prestigious. In the late eighteenth century there had been little to distinguish it from its neighbors, but by the early nineteenth century this scenic and conveniently situated community on the southwestern edge of the city had emerged as Boston's leading elite suburb.

The many prominent Bostonians who established country residences in Brookline in the early nineteenth century tended to settle in two fairly compact areas of the town—the elevated south central section, through which ran the old Sherborn Road (now Walnut Street) and neighboring Warren, Cottage and Goddard Streets (the area near the 1848 Brookline Reservoir), or, alternately, in the northeast corner of the community adjacent to Boston's Back Bay, the so-called Longwood–Cottage Farm district.

Among the first Bostonians to pick Brookline as a country retreat were the Cabots, Higginsons, Masons and Perkinses, families of great wealth and social prestige. Three early residents, George Cabot, Stephen Higginson and Jonathan Mason, were members of the so-called Essex Junto, an ultra-conservative faction that dominated Massachusetts politics at the beginning of the nineteenth century.

Brookline and Brighton voted on annexation on the same day, October 7, 1873, but made strikingly different decisions. Brookline had long been Boston's premier elite suburb and the town's voters were understandably reluctant to surrender their independence to the growing metropolis. *Courtesy of the Brighton-Allston Historical Society Archives.*

Another early settler of note was Thomas Handasyd Perkins, the leading China trade merchant of his day, who in 1799 acquired a sixty-seven-acre property on Cottage Street. Perkins's brothers and business partners, James and Samuel, also located nearby in the early years of the century. Later still, two of his sons-in-law, the merchant Samuel Cabot and the lawyer William H. Gardiner, established estates in the same general area. Other prominent families who established countryseats nearby included the Gardners, Philbricks, Sargents and Lees.

Brookline's other elite enclave, the Longwood–Cottage Farm district, was established from 1821 to 1851 chiefly by two wealthy Boston businessmen, David Sears and Amos Adams Lawrence.

While the owners of these country estates occupied the highest social position in Brookline, they composed only a tiny fraction of the town's overall population, of whom the great majority were ordinary farmers. And since the owners of these estates occupied their properties only in the warmer months of the year, they took little part in the management of the town's affairs.

A second and far more significant influx of well-to-do Bostonians entered Brookline between 1850 and 1870, a development that effected a political revolution in Brookline. The new residents were mostly Boston businessmen who had need to commute to their jobs and offices in the city on a daily basis. This influx of commuters was fostered by major improvements in the transportation network connecting Boston and Brookline that included the opening, in 1848, of the Brookline Branch Railroad linking Brookline Village with the downtown area; the construction, four years later, of the Charles River Railroad, an extension of the Brookline Branch into Chestnut Hill; the building, in 1851, through the heart of the town of Beacon Street; and, finally, the inauguration in 1859 of a horse-car line running from Brookline Village to Boston via Lower Roxbury and the South End.

Another key factor fostering the removal of these upper-class Bostonians to Brookline was a marked decline in the quality of life for residents of the inner city. Between 1840 and 1860 Boston experienced a virtual doubling of its population—from 93,000 to 178,000. As a result of the Irish potato famine of the late 1840s and early 1850s, the number of immigrants in Boston mushroomed, transforming the city's oldest neighborhoods—most notably the North End and Fort Hill districts—into congested, noisome, unhealthy slums. In addition, as Boston's commercial district expanded, the elegant residences that had once lined many downtown Boston streets were disappearing. In short, by the early 1850s the older parts of the city were no longer providing a suitable environment for middle- and upper-class families, causing them to flee to suburban locations, of which Brookline was a favorite destination.

Annexation Spurned

While a substantial number of Irish-Catholic immigrants also found their way into Brookline between 1846 and 1860, they came, more often than not, to work on the estates of Brookline's well-to-do residents. The Irish who could not be accommodated in this fashion were relegated to a crowded immigrant ghetto on the banks of the Muddy River just outside of Brookline Village, known as "The Marsh."

It should be emphasized that the post-1850 commuter element, which would eventually come to dominate Brookline, was different in several key respects from their elite predecessors. Though quite prosperous, they were not as wealthy as the earlier group. In addition, they were year-round residents, and as such, were much more interested in town government.

They also shared many of the values of the older elite element—admiring and seeking to emulate their lifestyle. Areas of cultural congruence included a common ethnic heritage (Anglo-American), a common religion (Protestantism) and a common social outlook. They also shared a pervasive sense of anxiety stemming from the rapid and destabilizing changes that were occurring in America from 1830 to 1860—changes in economic relationships, in the structure and function of the family and in the social and ethnic composition of society. No period of American history before or since has been more anxiety-ridden than the decades immediately preceding the Civil War.

This new commuter element quickly assumed leadership in Brookline. Under its direction, from 1850 to 1873, Brookline established public facilities and services that were comparable or superior to those in Boston—including well-constructed roadways, sidewalks, street lighting, a first-rate school system, handsome public buildings and ample police and fire protection. Moreover, the high-quality homes that the upper classes built in Brookline in these years gave the town a solid tax base that enabled it to make improvements without resorting either to heavy taxation or heavy borrowing.

Indicative of Brookline's lofty self-image at the time of the 1873 annexation vote is the following description from a leading resident, former U.S. Senator Robert C. Winthrop:

> I think that no one will dispute that Brookline was for a long time pre-eminent in the little cordon of towns which have so long constituted the exquisite environs of Boston...I speak of a half century...during which, certainly, Brookline, enjoyed a prestige for culture and beauty, which might almost have entitled her to that appellation of "a peculiar."

In only one respect was the elite suburb unable to furnish its citizens with services equal to Boston's—in the quantity and quality of its water supply. Boston's Cochituate Water System had been providing Boston neighborhoods with ample high-quality water since 1848. The pro-annexation forces contended that only through consolidation with Boston could Brookline procure a reliable supply of water.

Anti-annexationists countered this argument by questioning the capacity of the Cochituate System to meet Brookline's needs, claiming that its capacity was limited, and would shortly be too little to meet even Boston's water-supply needs.

But the most important factor shaping Brookline's 1873 rejection of annexation was the determination of its prosperous commuter class to preserve the edenic retreat it had created on the western edge of the city. This affluent, numerous and politically savvy element understood that annexation would rob it of its power to shape the future character of this unique town.

21

ANNEXATION EMBRACED
Brighton's 1873 Acceptance of Boston

On October 7, 1873, the voters of the independent towns of Brookline and Brighton made sharply contrasting decisions on the question of annexation to the City of Boston. While two-thirds of the voters of Brookline rejected a merger with the metropolis (for reasons spelled out in the previous chapter), fully 81 percent of Brighton's voters eagerly embraced the opportunity to join the city.

Why did these neighboring towns react so differently when presented with this momentous choice? The contrasting decisions stemmed from the very different economic and social character of these adjacent communities. Though once very similar (both had been farming towns before the American Revolution), by the early years of the nineteenth century, Brookline had become Boston's premier elite suburb, while Brighton had developed into one of the city's key industrial satellites.

The cornerstone of Brighton's industrial edifice was its livestock trade. This town at the western gateway to Boston was the principal cattle and slaughtering center of nineteenth-century New England. Thousands of head of livestock reached its stockyards and slaughtering facilities each week from distant points, some driven overland, some arriving by rail. In 1869 alone, 53,000 head of cattle, 144,000 hogs and 342,000 sheep arrived in Brighton.

Brighton also contained the largest concentration of slaughterhouses in New England—over forty of them in 1866. Other Brighton manufacturing establishments produced a wide range of animal byproducts, including varnish, lampblack, bone fertilizer, soap, oil, tallow, lard, whips, buttons and corset bones. Livestock-related enterprises served as the engine of the local economy.

More than any other local politician of the day State Senator William Wirt Warren was responsible for Brighton's 1873 ready acceptance of annexation to the City of Boston. In contrast to Brookline, which rejected annexation by a margin of two-to-one, more than four out of five Brighton voters approved it. *Courtesy of the Brighton-Allston Historical Society Archives.*

Annexation Embraced

While the great majority of the town's residents were dependent on the cattle and slaughtering trades—either directly or indirectly—for their livelihoods, these industries also emitted foul odors and generated waste products that were indiscriminately dumped into its watercourses. In 1866 public health expert Dr. Henry Clark described the waste disposal practices of the market town's forty-plus slaughterhouses as "prolific and provoking causes of disease."

For these reasons Bostonians looking for suburban locations in which to build homes were inclined to give Brighton a wide berth. Of all the towns around Boston, it had the lowest population of commuters.

Another barrier to residential development were the large numbers of drovers, cattle dealers, country farmers and itinerant merchants who poured into the town each week to attend the cattle market. The town contained a score of hotels for the accommodation of this transient element, hotels equipped with bars that dispensed as much liquor as the patrons cared to pay for, which tolerated disorderly and drunken behavior and furnished a haven for high-stake gambling.

The poor condition of Brighton's roads, its lack of street lighting and an almost complete absence of sewers also militated against suburban development. Believing that there was little point in investing the town's resources in roads over which droves of cattle were regularly driven, the town fathers spent very little money on highways. They also declined to invest in sewers, which might tend to undermine the freewheeling dumping practices upon which the slaughterhouse proprietors relied.

Though a relatively prosperous town, rather than endeavor to regulate its nuisance industries and thereby endanger its commercial and industrial economy, Brighton preferred to invest in high-quality public facilities—in a handsome Greek Revival town hall, a new brick grammar school, state-of-the-art firehouses and firefighting equipment and an elaborate fourteen-acre town cemetery. Such expenditures advertised the town's prosperity and protected its property without in any way threatening the well-being of the cattle and slaughtering trades.

The economic and political landscape of Brighton was transformed quite suddenly between 1870 and 1873—the four years that led up to the annexation vote—by two factors. One of these was a major technological breakthrough that revolutionized the meatpacking industry—the introduction of refrigerated cars on American rail lines. Once refrigerated cars came into service, cattle could be slaughtered nearer the source of supply. With the introduction of this technology the slaughtering industry of the Eastern United States began a slow but relentless decline.

Another factor that seriously threatened Brighton's cattle and slaughtering industries was the rise of a powerful public health movement in Massachusetts.

In 1869 the newly organized Massachusetts State Board of Health accused the Brighton slaughterhouses of sending tainted meat into Boston and demanded stricter regulation of the industry. The state board also pointed to Brighton's high mortality rate as evidence of the unhealthy disposal practices—a mortality rate equal to that of most crowded neighborhoods of Boston and higher than those of the nineteen largest cities and towns of the commonwealth.

To solve this problem, the state board urged the establishment of a single modern slaughtering facility somewhere near Boston—an abattoir—which all the butchers within a six-mile radius of the city would be required to use.

Brighton's more enterprising businessmen were quick to recognize the diminished prospects of the slaughtering trade—quick to appreciate that residential development now offered greater profit-making potential than the cattle and slaughtering trades.

At this point a group of Brighton businessmen took the initiative by establishing the Butcher's Slaughtering and Melting Association, the corporation that in 1872 built the sprawling Brighton Abattoir on the edge of the Charles River in North Brighton.

The business leaders who masterminded the transformation of Brighton from 1870 to 1873—beginning with the abattoir scheme—were well-to-do men who had made their fortunes, either directly or indirectly, from the town's cattle and slaughtering trades: Benjamin Franklin Ricker, Horace Jordan and Horace Baxter, all slaughterhouse proprietors; State Senator William Wirt Warren, the favorite lawyer and politico of the slaughterhouse proprietors; and George Wilson, a hotel keeper and speculator. All of them owned substantial real estate, which they expected would appreciate in value as a result of the measures they supported.

Prior to filing the legislation that created the abattoir corporation, this same group of businessmen—later referred to as "The Brighton Ring"—managed to seize control of Brighton's Board of Selectmen and Board of Health. In the four years that followed, they dominated the political life of the town.

The transformation of Brighton from an industrial town to a commuter suburb was accomplished in three broad steps between 1870 and 1873. First, the town's slaughterhouses were closed down and its butchers were forced into the abattoir, thereby opening previously fouled acreage to suburban development. Then, a massive public works program was inaugurated with the object of making Brighton more attractive to would-be commuters. In the four years leading up to the annexation referendum, Brighton spent some $500,000 on improved roads, curbs, sidewalks, sewers and street lighting. Additional sums were spent on public facilities, including a new public library, a new grammar school and a new firehouse. The "Brighton Ring" also used its control of town meetings for private profit, frequently selling the town parcels of land at greatly inflated prices.

The impact of this orgy of spending on the town's finances was, I would suggest, intentionally staggering. Brighton's revenue stream in the four years under consideration totaled only $438,000, but its level of spending reached an incredible $1,560,000, four times what it received. The difference could be made up only one way—by heavy borrowing. Between 1870 and 1873, Brighton's town debt increased by 800 percent! If Brighton had remained an independent town after 1873, its residents would have been obliged to pay substantially higher taxes.

Members of the ring meanwhile filed the legislation that authorized Brighton's annexation to Boston. In building the town's huge indebtedness, they laid the groundwork for the annexation decision of October 7, 1873. Allow Boston to annex Brighton, they advised the town's electors, and the metropolis would automatically absorb Brighton's potentially crippling debt.

As the debt rose between 1870 and 1873, the opposition to annexation, which had been fairly strong in 1870, steadily eroded. As early as December 1872, nearly a year before the annexation vote, a majority of those attending a town meeting approved instructing Brighton's representatives in the state legislature to "use their utmost efforts in behalf of annexation." A rising tax rate, coupled with a prospect of further sharp increases, had reconciled the great majority of Brighton's voters to union with Boston.

Thus when the question was finally put to the voters of Brighton in the fall of 1873, they embraced annexation by an overwhelming vote of 622 to 133.

22

ALLSTON'S HISTORIC BEACON
TROTTING PARK

Few realize that the extensive Beacon Park Freight Yard in Allston was named for an older institution, the Beacon Trotting Park, which occupied the site from the mid-1860s to the early 1890s.

Beacon Park, one of the pioneer racetracks in New England, was founded in 1864 as a half-mile-long course for sulky racing and was at first called Riverside Park.

Other early trotting parks near Boston included the South End Driving Park (1852), Old Cambridge Park in North Cambridge (1857), Franklin Park in Saugus (1857) and Mystic Park in South Medford (1866).

The founders of these early racetracks almost always established a public house nearby, which offered their patrons overnight accommodation as well as opportunities for drinking, gambling and other "diversions."

In the case of Riverside Trotting Park, the public house was the Riverside Hotel, which was situated at the northwest corner of Cambridge and North Harvard Streets. The Riverside Hotel soon became a favorite resort of Boston's racing and betting crowd.

The earliest manager of this hostelry, Samuel Emerson (who may also have been the initial owner of the park), was a leading figure in the early history of New England trotting parks and had previously managed Saugus's Franklin Park.

Interestingly, the neighborhood across Cambridge Street from Riverside Park, where the hotel was situated—an area called Prattville after Isaac

Pratt, a major Allston landowner—contained Allston-Brighton's largest concentration of black families, drawn to the location by the employment opportunities associated with the trotting park.

Riverside Park was a great popular success chiefly because of its proximity to Boston. Bostonians reached the park by three routes. Those driving out in private horse-drawn carriages used the Brighton Road (Commonwealth and Brighton Avenues) and then Cambridge Street to reach the park entrance. For those without private conveyances, public transportation was available. The more affluent element utilized the Boston and Albany Railroad, boarding its trains at the B&A's downtown depot on Beach Street for the twenty-minute ride to the Allston Depot, which lay a scant quarter-mile south of the park's entrance. Less affluent patrons used the much slower but inexpensive horsecars that ran from Bowdoin Square in the West End over the West Boston Bridge into Cambridge, and then over the Cambridge Street Bridge to the park entrance.

At the height of the trotting park's popularity in the 1880s, one source tells us, horsecars lined up outside the main gate on racing day to accommodate the many thousands of patrons in need of transportation back to the city.

The first public trainer to locate at Riverside Park, a major figure in the history of the American trotting horse, was the renowned J.J. "Uncle Jock" Bowen. Bowen ran the very first race that was decided over the course.

In 1865 Uncle Jock also set a world trotting record at Riverside Park for a twenty-mile distance with a horse named Captain McGowan—accomplishing this feat in an amazing fifty-six minutes and twenty-five seconds, a record not broken for several decades thereafter. This demonstration of trotting speed was witnessed by an estimated five to six thousand amazed spectators. As racing historian Peter Welsh has written of this signal event: "Betting was heavy, and in the stands many people stated loudly that no horse could accomplish the feat." Bowen and the great trotter nonetheless performed the task with seeming ease, and Captain McGowan's delighted owners collected a purse of $5,500.

In 1869 Riverside Trotting Park changed hands when it was purchased for $39,000 by real estate speculator and horse racing enthusiast John A. Sawyer, who undertook to enlarge the facility into a mile-long course, a measure requiring the approval of the Town of Brighton. The petition generated a lively controversy. Horse racing, of course, attracted gamblers and other disreputable elements, which caused the town's beleaguered middle class great concern.

Opponents of the enlarged track hired local attorney William Wirt Warren, the town's leading political figure, and Edward Dexter Sohier, the great Boston criminal lawyer, whose Allston home lay directly across the

Beacon Park racetrack, as it looked about 1890. The park was located on the site of the present Beacon Park Freight Yard in North Allston. A popular resort of Boston's racing and gambling fraternity on the main horsecar line that ran from Boston's West End via Cambridge into Brighton-Allston, it attracted tens of thousands of visitors each week during the racing season. *Courtesy of the Brighton-Allston Historical Society Archives.*

B&A tracks from the park, to represent them at a public hearing held before the Brighton Board of Selectmen on January 5 and 7, 1870.

At the first session, eight adjacent landowners spoke in favor of the Sawyer proposal, apparently believing that the expansion of the park would increase the value of their property. On January 7, the opponents responded. Warren, in his opening remarks, noted that "the names of the men signing the remonstrance represented about a million and a half of taxable real estate in the town, or about one fourth of the total taxable valuation," while the eight landowners who had testified in favor of the proposal owned property valued at only $300,000. Warren contended that an immense amount of injury would be done to Brighton by the proposed expansion. It would "depreciate the value of real estate, and the associations connected with the park would drive away the residents from their valuable estates to other towns, which would deprive the town of a larger amount of taxes than would ever be received from the park."

Most of the testimony against the park emphasized the themes of property depreciation and "social annoyances." Crowds of ten to twelve thousand would be drawn into Brighton on racing days, it was maintained. Two state police detectives testified that "a large number of professional gamblers and pickpockets were in the habit of visiting Riverside" and that "if a mile track were licensed there it would draw a larger attendance of all classes of people than it had previously done. Gambling implements had been seized by them at Riverside," they emphasized.

The selectmen rejected Sawyer's petition, but that did not settle the matter. The town's business element rallied to the defense of Sawyer. In later testimony before the legislature's committee on towns, William C. Strong, Brighton's leading horticulturalist and an advocate of residential development, noted that "the selectmen refused to allow the race course there, but a town meeting was called which included all the roughs of the town, and it required the selectmen to locate the park." This town meeting approved the expansion of the trotting park by the considerable margin of 149 to 41 votes, evidencing the power that the town's commercial interests wielded in the political life of the community.

In 1870 Sawyer converted Riverside Park into a mile-long course, giving the expanded facility the new name, Beacon Park. Sawyer's alterations, which cost the entrepreneur $50,000, included twenty-five new carriage stalls for "gentlemen attendees," where the more valuable carriages could be kept under lock and key; a completely new track; a new judge's platform and a much expanded spectators' stand, capable of accommodating 2,500 patrons, with spaces provided underneath for the less affluent. The sections of the mile-long course were given names—"Brookside" was applied to the portion that extended from the judge's stand to the edge of the Charles River (paralleling Smelt Inlet, the historic boundary between Brighton and Brookline), the name "Roadside" was applied to the portion of the track that ran along Cambridge Street while the section extending from Cambridge Street to the finish line was dubbed "Homestretch."

Sawyer owned Beacon Park only briefly, however. In 1872 the wily speculator sold the trotting park to its last owners, Eben Jordan and Charles Marsh, owners of the Jordan Marsh Department Store, for the sum of $169,000, thereby doubling his investment in three short years.

For the next two decades, Beacon Park continued attracting substantial patronage and was the scene of many notable racing events. The two most significant were the Great Stallion Race for the championship of the United States, which the trotter Smuggler won in 1874, and an 1880 race in which

St. Julien set a new world speed record for a mile-long run, of 2 minutes 13¼ seconds. A Brighton hotel, the St. Julien House at Market and North Beacon Streets in North Brighton, was later named in honor of this famous racehorse.

A particularly interesting facet of Beacon Park's last decade was its use by Buffalo Bill's Wild West Show while in Boston. William F. Cody, a former scout in the Sioux-Cheyenne country of the northern plains, started his Wild West Show in 1883, touring the country and thrilling audiences with the reenactment of exciting incidents from life on the plains. The choice of Beacon Park in Allston as a venue for this colorful event was almost certainly related to its proximity to the Brighton Stockyards, which had just relocated from Brighton Center to North Brighton. There the great showman's horses and buffalo could be quartered between performances.

Some thirty-five years ago, ninety-five-year-old Allston-Brighton historian and raconteur Tom McVey remembered an occasion from his youth when a herd of buffalo, part of Buffalo Bill's menagerie, were being herded down Lincoln Street on their way to Beacon Park. As McVey recalled, a big black dog startled the buffalo, causing them to scatter and "run wild all over North Brighton. They were rounded up," he noted, "by Buffalo Bill's Indians on horseback. These were not moving picture Indians," McVey emphasized, "but the real McCoy."

Beacon Park ceased to exist in the early 1890s, when Messrs. Jordan and Marsh sold the property to the Boston and Albany Railroad for conversion to a freight yard. It then comprised sixty acres. While some of this parcel was later taken for the building of Storrow Drive and the Massachusetts Turnpike Extension, most of the footprint of the original Beacon Park Raceway lies within the appropriately named Beacon Park Freight Yard of our day.

23

BOSTON'S FIRST ELECTRIC STREETCAR RIDE BEGINS IN BRIGHTON-ALLSTON

One of the most important events in the transportation history of Boston, the first electric streetcar ride, emanated from Allston-Brighton in December 1888. Boston was not the first city in America to introduce electric streetcars. That distinction belongs to Baltimore, which acquired a system in 1885, but Boston was not far behind.

Since the late 1850s, Boston had been served by a network of horse-drawn lines running on rails, which by the 1880s employed eight thousand animals. Horsecars, as these vehicles were called, had some serious disadvantages. First, the draft animals had to be fed and to be cared for, which involved considerable expense. In addition, the cars moved slowly and extra teams had to be employed to get them over steep grades. Also, overworked horses sometimes died in harness. And finally, epidemics of equine fever forced occasional service shutdowns.

And there was, of course, the problem of disposing of the huge quantity of dung that the horses deposited on the city's streets. The average droppings per horse amounted to ten pounds a day and much of it was left to dry and mix with the air. Some historians attribute a rise in the incidence of tuberculosis in nineteenth-century American cities to the dried airborne dung that residents were breathing.

Electric streetcars, by contrast, were relatively pollution-free. They also ran much faster than horsecars (ten to fifteen miles per hour, as compared to five to six for the animal-powered vehicles). Also, they could carry more passengers per trip, making it possible to offer the public cheaper fares. And finally, the electric system enjoyed important long-term economic advantages, for once the initial high installation costs were met, there were no heavy, long-term expenses to be borne.

The first step toward the introduction of electric streetcars in Boston came in 1887, when Brookline developer Henry M. Whitney consolidated virtually all of the horsecar companies of Boston into the West End Street Railway Company, which in 1897 became the Boston Elevated Railway.

Whitney was fascinated by the possibility of substituting electric power for horsepower. With that goal in mind he visited Richmond, Virginia, where experimentation with electric power was under way. There he made the acquaintance of inventor-engineer Frank J. Sprague and decided to award the Sprague Electric Railway and Motor Company a contract to electrify a line running from Allston's Braintree Street to Park Square in the Back Bay. Branches of the first electric streetcar line also ran up Beacon Street from Coolidge Corner to Cleveland Circle and from the Allston powerhouse to a car barn in Oak Square.

How did the people of Brighton-Allston respond to the proposal that an electric streetcar line be established in their community? Local businessmen and landowners were quite supportive. Samuel Hano, who owned a large bookbindery in Allston, as well as some half-million square feet of local real estate, gave the project a powerful endorsement, as did Horace Jordan, a former Brighton selectman and co-founder of the Brighton Abattoir.

An electric streetcar outside of the original Oak Square Car Barn (on the site of the present Oak Square YMCA) on Washington Street in the 1890s. The Oak Square Car Barn was the point of origin of the very first electric streetcar trip in Boston, which occurred on December 1, 1888. *Courtesy of the Brighton-Allston Historical Society Archives.*

Meanwhile Henry Lee and Henry M. Stanwood of Brookline circulated a petition to require the West End Street Railway Company to put all of its electric lines into underground conduits. Regrettably businessmen Hano and Jordan refused to support this effort, fearing that the added cost of an underground system might jeopardize the electrification project. In the end the Boston Board of Aldermen permitted the company to erect utility poles in Allston-Brighton, while requiring that the Back Bay lines be placed underground.

There was apparently no organized opposition to the electrification proposal in Brighton-Allston. The local paper, the *Brighton Item*, predicted that electric streetcar service would lead to "the commencement of another boom in the already well-inflated real estate interests of the district," and also that a second electric line would soon be built on Chestnut Hill Avenue to spur the development of that section of town. In the latter prediction the paper was, of course, quite mistaken.

In the fall of 1888, a power station and car barn were constructed on Braintree Street near the Allston Depot. On December 1, the *Item* noted that the recently completed power station's most notable feature was a hundred-foot-tall chimney. The facility contained two Armington and Sims pattern two-hundred-horsepower engines, driven by four Edison dynamos, having a maximum pressure of five hundred volts apiece. These were operated by three horizontal tubular boilers, furnished by the Jarvis Engineering Company.

An electric streetcar on Cambridge Street, Allston approaching Union Square, about 1900. *Courtesy of the Brighton-Allston Historical Society Archives.*

The inauguration of electric streetcar service in Boston is traditionally dated from a formal ceremony held on December 31, 1888, when an electric-powered car traveled from the Allston car barn to Boston's Park Square. My research reveals, however, that the first trip on the line actually occurred a month earlier, on December 1, 1888, consisting of a test run from Oak Square to Allston, and then out to Beacon Street and back. A description of this initial trip appeared in the *Item* on December 8, 1888:

> *Early in the afternoon a handsomely painted car was drawn by two large gray horses from the company's shops to Oak Square, and the news spread quite rapidly that a car was to be run over the road by electricity. Owing to trifling fixings the car did not leave Oak Square for some time, but at 5:30 o'clock the people of the central portion of the district saw the first car run by the new system. The car moved along with great ease and at a comfortable speed to Allston where the Harvard Avenue line was traveled over to Beacon Street. The distance on Beacon Street was traversed to the new bridge, after which a return trip was made. At Beacon Street a spurt was made and the car traveled along at a rate of some 15 miles an hour.*
>
> *The utility of the system received about as thorough a test as is likely to be put between Lake and Foster Streets, and the feat was accomplished with little apparent effort. The stopping and starting is a marvel of perfection, the stop being made in a surprisingly short distance, while the start is practically immediate. The time of running necessitated the introduction of light and the incandescents used for this purpose lent no small amount of attractiveness to the pleasant sight.*
>
> *It is perhaps needless to say that a large number of spectators were out in force to witness the trial, and they appeared as much pleased as those directly interested. The car presented a novel sight with the electric flashes flying from wheels and wires.*
>
> *The car was operated by Mr. Sprague whose name the system bears, and quite a number of officials enjoying the trip.*

Within a few months, the West End Street Railway was operating twenty-eight miles of electrified track in the downtown area, Brookline, Brighton and Cambridge.

All the West End Street Railway's power at this early stage was supplied from the Braintree Street power station in Allston. Later additional stations were built in East Cambridge and at Harrison Avenue in Roxbury—the latter becoming the system's central power facility.

24

NORTH ALLSTON
The Early Years

Northi Allston's attractive St. Anthony's Church neighborhood is one of the best-kept secrets in Allston. The transportation corridors that border the district—the Massachusetts Turnpike to the south, Everett Street to the west and Western Avenue to the north—effectually camouflage this handsome residential enclave from public view.

During the colonial era, the area formed a part of the extensive Sparhawk estate. At the center of the Sparhawk property stood an old mansion house, the home in the pre-Revolutionary era of Samuel Sparhawk, that was situated about 150 feet south of the present-day intersection of Antwerp Street and Western Avenue.

Samuel Sparhawk's wife was the sister of Colonel Thomas Gardner, another major Allston landowner. Mortally wounded at the battle of Bunker Hill, Gardner was carried to the Sparhawk Mansion, where he died sixteen days later. Brighton historian J.P.C. Winship tells us that George Washington attended the funeral services for Colonel Gardner, which "were held at the Sparhawk Mansion on Western Avenue."

As the second-highest-ranking American officer to lose his life in that historic battle, this Revolutionary martyr is commemorated locally by Gardner Street and the Thomas Gardner Elementary School. In addition, the city of Gardner, Massachusetts, was named for him.

About 1810, when the Sparhawk property was subdivided and sold, the mansion and the western part of the estate were purchased by Edmund Rice, who had recently moved to Brighton from Wayland, Massachusetts. Rice converted the old mansion into a hotel and tavern, which became a regular stop for the stagecoaches that ran between Cambridge and interior locations.

The impact of Harvard College upon the northern part of Allston-Brighton, usually thought of as a modern phenomenon, was already evident in Edmund Rice's time, for as J.P.C. Winship wrote, Rice's Tavern was "a favorite resort for the officers and students of Harvard College," especially after Cambridge prohibited the sale of liquor within its boundaries. The tavern was taken down in the 1890s at the time of the construction of Antwerp Street.

The northeasterly portion of the Sparhawk estate (including the land upon which the St. Anthony's Church neighborhood now stands) was acquired in 1810 by Aaron and Abner Everett, who engaged in farming on the site for many decades thereafter. The Everett farms encompassed most of the land bounded by present-day Everett Street, Western Avenue, Franklin and Holton Streets. Everett Street, which was put through in 1846, was named for this early family. The Everett house stood on the southern side of Western Avenue near present-day Westford Street (which originally bore the name Everett Square).

In the colonial period, much of North Allston and North Brighton belonged to the Sparhawk family. Here we see the Samuel Sparhawk Mansion, which stood near the intersection of present-day Western Avenue and Antwerp Street. George Washington visited this house in June 1775 to attend the funeral of Samuel Sparhawk's brother-in-law, the Revolutionary War hero Colonel Thomas Gardner. The house was taken down in the late nineteenth century. *Courtesy of the Brighton-Allston Historical Society Archives.*

In the late 1850s, the Everetts began selling off portions of their land for residential development, though they retained ownership of some local acreage as late as the 1860s.

Most of the land in the neighborhood was still devoted to farming until 1875, when the first comprehensive map of the neighborhood was published. Since the quality of North Allston's soil was of a particularly high order, this acreage was utilized chiefly for the cultivation of fruit and vegetables for the Boston market. The farms of North Allston were quite close to Boston and were moreover linked to the metropolis by a superior network of roads, bridges and the nearby Boston and Worcester Railroad (dating from 1834). Thus, it made good economic sense for local farmers to specialize in the cultivation of perishable commodities for the city's growing population.

The federal agricultural schedule for 1860 identifies the North Allston farms of that day as belonging to Patrick Colby, Nathan Tucker, Abner Everett, Aaron Everett, John C. Scott, Abel Rice, Frank H. Coolidge and Emery Willard—farms which comprised, in aggregate, more than three hundred acres. Two of the most interesting of these establishments were the strawberry farms of Abel Rice and John C. Scott, both of which lay adjacent to Everett Street.

In 1836 Abel Rice, a cousin of Edmund Rice, and a former Brighton Center schoolmaster, purchased eight acres of land near the intersection of Everett and Holton Streets. Here the farmer and schoolmaster constructed a Greek Revival–style residence with an ell for schoolrooms, a structure that still stands at 205 Everett Street. Rice devoted his North Allston acreage to the cultivation of strawberries. He is said to have introduced the very first strawberries to the Boston market. Abel was succeeded in this business by his sons, Abel Jr. and William H. Rice, who carried on strawberry farming there until about 1900.

John C. Scott, who had once been gardener to the great merchant prince Peter Chardon Brooks, came to North Allston in 1840, purchasing an eleven-acre property on the western side of Everett Street, near the present Brighton Mills Shopping Center. Here he produced strawberry seedlings of great merit, including the Scott Seedling, Brighton Pine and Lady of the Lake. This highly successful business was later carried on by his sons, John, James and George Scott, who continued to operate the business well into the second decade of the twentieth century.

Residential development in the neighborhood was stimulated by a number of factors. The proximity of the Boston and Albany Railroad and its Allston Depot fostered house construction by Boston commuters. One could reach Boston's commercial district from this neighborhood by train in about twenty minutes. The Boston commuters who resided in the neighborhood in 1875 included S.A. Harrington, an inspector at the Boston Customs House; Isaac N. Tucker, who ran a leading plumbing supply house; John Davenport Jr., a tobacconist; Noah Colman, a dealer in hats; Jonathan D. Wright, a theater manager; D.C. Robbins, a manufacturer; and A.L. Smart, proprietor of a carpet cleaning establishment.

One of the earliest commuting families to locate in the area were the Davenports. In 1852 John Davenport Sr. (1802–1897) moved his large family from Purchase Street in the Fort Hill section of Boston to land he had acquired from the Everetts and built 21 Holton Street, a large Greek Revival–style residence. John was fifty years of age when he moved out to Allston, a successful contractor whose Boston buildings included the city's largest warehouse. He was attracted to the neighborhood by the richness of its soil, for he was also an amateur horticulturalist.

John had two sons, the previously mentioned John Jr., a prosperous tobacco merchant, and Samuel, who was just twelve at the time of the move. Samuel especially liked the new neighborhood near the tidal Charles River, where he could indulge his passions for hunting, fishing, skating and boating. Samuel later followed in his father's footsteps, becoming a successful architect and builder. Much of the Sparhawk Street neighborhood, behind Brighton's District 14 Police Station, was designed and built by Samuel N. Davenport.

The Davenports constructed several residences in the St. Anthony's neighborhood over the years. By 1890, members of the family owned eight houses on Holton, Brentwood, Aldie and Athol Streets.

Another family that played a key role in the development of this neighborhood were the Tuckers. Moses D. Tucker was a retail provisions merchant, with offices in Boston. His son, the previously mentioned Isaac N., ran a Boston plumbing supply business. The family hailed from Raymond, New Hampshire. Since Raymond Street was laid out across the Tucker property, it seems likely it was named for that New Hampshire town. Moses Tucker's house, a Second Empire mansard at 134 Franklin Street, dating probably from the 1860s, was one of the neighborhood's most elaborate residences. Members of the Tucker family built several houses along Franklin and Raymond Streets and on nearby Appian Way.

Much of the development that occurred in the neighborhood between 1850 and 1900, however, was for the benefit of the owners and employees of local businesses.

As the facilities of the Boston and Albany Railroad expanded (by the 1870s it was the largest taxpayer and largest employer in the town), railroad employees took up residence nearby, especially along Lincoln and Adams (now Adamson) Streets, adjacent to the B&A railroad's car repair shops.

The neighborhood's nearness to the Brighton Abattoir and stockyards in North Brighton also made it a convenient place of residence for meat dealers and butchers. In the late nineteenth century, these were the single largest occupational groups in the neighborhood.

Cordage manufacturers James and Leonard Arkerson, whose establishments stood on the north side of Western Avenue (James's ropewalk at 299 Western Avenue was over a thousand feet long), also built houses in the St. Anthony's neighborhood. James lived at 306 Western Avenue, on the corner of Everett Street.

By the late 1880s, the area was poised for a second spurt of development, including the 1895 construction of the handsome St. Anthony's Church.

25

North Allston After 1885

The period from 1885 to 1910 was one of rapid residential and industrial development for North Allston. The first major new industrial facility to establish itself in the general neighborhood was the Sewall and Day cordage factory, which opened in 1889, the same year that electric streetcar service was instituted between Boston and the nearby Braintree Street car barns. By 1896 streetcar service also existed along Western Avenue.

The Sewall and Day complex sat on a twenty-three-acre parcel of land at the southwest corner of Western Avenue and Everett Streets, acreage that is now largely occupied by the Brighton Mills Shopping Mall. Founded by Benjamin Sewall and Moses Day in 1834, Sewall and Day was a major Boston manufacturer. Before moving to Allston it had occupied land on the margin of the old Back Bay where the Museum of Fine Arts stands today. Property values in that neighborhood were rising so rapidly by the 1880s that the owners decided to sell the Fenway acreage and move to less valuable land in North Allston.

The company's immense North Allston facility included a 1,940-foot-long wooden ropewalk that stretched from Western Avenue all the way back to Lincoln Street. Paralleling this ropewalk, about 200 feet to the east were two large brick mills, each measuring 300 by 105 feet. Between the ropewalk and the mills stood several smaller structures, including a machine shop, a boiler house and a tar shop.

The Sewall and Day complex was designed by the firm of Cutting and Bishop, one of New England's leading industrial architects.

North Allston After 1885

The opening of the Sewall and Day factory, with its many job opportunities, probably accounts for the construction shortly thereafter of a large apartment complex, three groups of brick duplexes, at numbers 70 to 76, 80 to 86, and 88 to 98 Raymond Street. The developer was John F. Mead, after whom Mead Street was named.

In its heyday, Sewall and Day (renamed the Standard Rope and Twine Company after its merger with two other companies in 1893), utilized the services of as many as six hundred workers, and was long North Allston's largest employer. The cordage firm went out of business in 1912, owing to the pressure of foreign competition.

In 1921, after standing empty for several years, the complex was purchased by the New England Spun Silk Company, a manufacturer of high-grade silk yarn. Another major employer of local residents, New England Spun Silk closed its doors in 1963, the structures thereafter accommodating a wide range of commercial uses until demolished in 1996.

Another significant development was the building, in 1891–92, of the Everett Street Bridge, constructed by order of the State Superior Court, which had deemed the at-grade railroad crossing at Everett Street to be a serious hazard. This bridge opened on June 4, 1892.

An even more hazardous crossing point on the Boston and Albany Railroad tracks lay at Franklin Street where pedestrian traffic was quite heavy and many fatalities had occurred over the years. The problem was dealt with in 1894 by the construction of a tunnel under the tracks for the convenience of local residents.

The next major building project in the neighborhood was the construction of St. Anthony's Church, completed in 1894–95. Father Anthony J. Rossi, pastor of St. Columbkille's Church, was largely responsible for the building of this handsome Romanesque Revival edifice, intended as a local annex to St. Columbkille's, then Allston-Brighton's only Catholic church. The architect, Swiss immigrant Franz Joseph Untersee, was a leading church designer whose other works include the towers at Roxbury's Mission Church, the Mission Church High School and St. Lawrence's Church in Brookline.

The groundbreaking ceremony at St. Anthony's took place on Sunday, September 16, 1894, at 2:30 p.m., when a long procession accompanied by a brass band wound its way from the parent church on Market Street to the construction site on Holton Street where a platform, decorated with the American and papal flags, had been erected for the visiting dignitaries. Boston Archbishop John Williams officiated.

Named St. Anthony of Padua Church, the edifice was completed in the fall of 1895 and was dedicated on November 24, 1895. St. Anthony's

Church was at first staffed by priests from St. Columbkille's. However, the congregation's steady growth led to its separation from the parent church in 1899, with Father Patrick J. Hally as its first pastor.

The first public school to be built in the neighborhood, the Everett School, was constructed in 1873, and stood at the northeast corner of Athol and Brentwood Streets. Designed by Brighton-born architect George Fuller, this wooden two-story structure housed the very first kindergarten ever to exist in a Boston public school, established by the Brighton School Committee the year before the town's annexation to the city. Unfortunately, Boston almost immediately closed down this pioneer facility.

By the turn of the century, the population of the northern section of Allston-Brighton was growing so rapidly that the three schoolhouses of the district were terribly overcrowded. So congested had these buildings become that the school department was forced to install portable classrooms and to rent nearby storefronts to accommodate the overflow.

With the opening of the Thomas Gardner School in 1905, such makeshift arrangements were abandoned. The handsome new brick schoolhouse, designed by the firm of Stickney and Austin, is especially notable for the decorative richness of its auditorium. Since the Gardner School was placed on the same lot as the Everett School, the older building had to be moved to the northern end of the parcel, where it continued to function as an annex of the larger building for many years.

This was the largest of the several schoolhouses that after 1905 composed the new Gardner School District, which served the northern part of the community. These included the William Wirt Warren School on Waverly Street, the Auburn School on Lothrop Street and the North Harvard School on North Harvard Street.

In all, the new Gardner School District contained fifteen hundred students, six hundred of whom were attending Gardner. Since the population of the district continued to expand, in 1923 the city was obliged to add a new wing to the Gardner School.

Several more Catholic buildings were constructed in the neighborhood in the 1899 to 1930 period. These included a church rectory for St. Anthony's, built when the church became a separate parish in 1899; St. Anthony's Parochial School, dating from 1913; and St. Anthony's Convent, dating from about 1930. Interestingly, all of these Catholic buildings occupied acreage that had once formed part of the Rice and Scott strawberry farms.

The area that lay just north of the neighborhood, between Western Avenue and the Charles River, experienced major changes in the 1897 to

The handsome Romanesque-style St. Anthony's Church was built at the northwest corner of Holton and Athol Streets in 1894–95 on a design of the noted architect Franz Joseph Untersee. St. Anthony's Church and the neighboring St. Anthony's School long served as the social focal points of this mostly Roman Catholic neighborhood. *Courtesy of the Brighton-Allston Historical Society Archives.*

North Allston's Gardner Elementary School, dating from 1905, and to the rear, the earlier Everett School, dating from 1873, the site of the first kindergarten in Boston. For many years the Everett School served as an annex to the larger building. *Courtesy of the Brighton-Allston Historical Society Archives.*

1927 period that strengthened the residential character of the St. Anthony's neighborhood.

In the late 1890s, the City of Boston purchased a fifteen-acre parcel near the northwest corner of Western Avenue and North Harvard Street and established the North Brighton Playground, later renamed the William F. Smith Playground.

Then Harvard University began transforming the acreage it owned along the Charles River into one of the most attractive stretches along that watercourse. The first Harvard buildings to be constructed on the margin of the river in North Allston were built between 1897 and 1903. These included the Carey Cage athletic facility and the Newell Boat House, both built in the late 1890s.

Next came the massive Harvard Stadium, dating from 1903, which enjoys the distinction of being both the world's first massive structure of reinforced concrete and the first large arena for college athletics to be built in the United States. Then, between 1925 and 1927, the Harvard School of Business Administration took up residence on the Allston shore in a handsome grid of Georgian Revival–style buildings facing the Charles, which were tied to the parent campus by the handsome Weeks footbridge. These improvements will be dealt with in greater detail in chapter 29, entitled "Harvard on the Charles."

Another development that had an indirect but important influence upon North Allston was the damming of the mouth of the Charles River in 1908. With the exclusion of the tides from the estuary, most of the industrial and commercial activity on the edge of the river ended, and the process of conversion of the river shoreline to recreational uses was given added impetus.

26

THE EMERGENCE OF ABERDEEN

The Aberdeen section of Brighton, which lies just outside of Cleveland Circle, contains some of the finest turn-of-the-twentieth-century architecture in the city of Boston. Unfortunately, this unique concentration of high-style Medieval Revival, Queen Anne, Shingle and Colonial Revival edifices experienced a steady erosion for many years at the hands of insensitive developers and absentee landlords.

In 2002 concerned residents, working under the auspices of the local neighborhood association with help from the Boston Landmarks Commission and the Brighton-Allston Historical Society, secured the designation of Aberdeen as a City of Boston Architectural Conservation District, which will in future serve to protect this unique neighborhood from inappropriate alterations to its architecture and landscape.

Aberdeen developed quite late, emerging only after 1887, which accounts for the high degree of architectural unity that exists there. As late as 1875, when the first detailed map of the southeast corner of the community appeared, there were only a handful of houses in the area.

In earlier times, when farming was still the primary occupation of Brighton's population, this corner of the town had scant appeal. In 1889 the *Brighton Item* described the area as one of "vast acres of high, gravel land which have never produced anything for their owners but grass and tax-bills."

Another factor that discouraged early development was the existence of two noxious industries in the area. One of these, the Curtis and Boynton Slaughterhouse, which stood a little west of the present intersection of

Sutherland Road and Commonwealth Avenue, was described in these terms in an 1866 government report:

> *The largest* [slaughtering] *business in Brighton at the time of the Civil War* [Curtis and Boynton] *employed from thirty to fifty men and required a stable of about 25 work horses to do the trucking with frequent employment for hired teams. This business was that of slaughtering hogs, rendering lard, and manufacturing lard oil. The offal from the slaughterhouse was usually piled up out in the open air and quite often not covered with anything, and was thus allowed to decay.*

Another odiferous slaughterhouse, belonging to Joseph L. White, stood near the entrance of the present Beacon Street Massachusetts Bay Transit Authority (MBTA) car barns, opposite Applebee's restaurant in Cleveland Circle.

Slaughterhouses, of course, make singularly unpleasant neighbors, so it is understandable that potential commuters had little wish to locate near such facilities.

The prerequisites for high-quality residential development in Aberdeen began to emerge only after the Civil War. First came the building of the nearby Chestnut Hill Reservoir, a holding facility for Boston's water supply, which was constructed between 1866 and 1870. The completed reservoir was a magnificent visual and recreational amenity that added greatly to the physical charms of the neighborhood.

Another helpful development came in 1867 when the Charles River Branch Railroad, which had been built through the area in 1852, opened a depot just east of the present Cleveland Circle Theater. The depot was built to accommodate the large numbers of workers employed by the builders of the reservoir. This line still exists today as the Riverside streetcar line.

The closing of the two local slaughterhouses in the early 1870s eliminated a major obstacle to quality residential development in the neighborhood. However, such development did not begin for another fifteen years. Transportation factors were largely responsible.

One must bear in mind that the area was quite remote from downtown and that the only major roadway connecting this southeastern corner of Brighton to the metropolis, Beacon Street, was then a fifty-foot-wide unpaved country lane. Also, despite the existence of a local railroad depot, the passenger rates on the Charles River line were relatively high, which discouraged commuting. In addition, hundreds of acres of more conveniently situated building lots were available closer at hand, in Boston's developing Back Bay. Moreover, in 1873 the nation slipped into a major depression lasting several years, which retarded the local real estate market.

While Allston-Brighton's Commonwealth Avenue was laid out in the late 1880s, it did not begin to experience significant development until after streetcar service was introduced in 1909. Here we see Commonwealth Avenue near Wallingford Road, in the Aberdeen neighborhood, as it appeared about 1910 before the area had experienced any development. *Courtesy of the Brighton-Allston Historical Society Archives.*

In 1886 the greatest impediment to development was removed when Henry M. Whitney, the president of the West End Street Railway Company, and a major owner of Beacon Street real estate, hired renowned landscape architect Frederick Law Olmsted to widen and improve Beacon Street. Over the next two years, Olmsted replaced the rough country lane with a spectacular 160-foot-wide paved Parisian-style boulevard. Most of this work on this grand avenue was completed by the end of 1887.

Whitney, the enterprising Brookline entrepreneur, also installed an electric streetcar line on the reconstructed roadway. As Cynthia Zaitzevsky wrote in her history of the Boston park system: "The improved Beacon Street proved enormously profitable for Brookline through increased tax revenues, as well as for Whitney, and it was generally regarded as a triumph."

The Olmsted firm had also been hired by the City of Boston to devise a plan for a second grand avenue in the eastern part of Brighton to link lower Commonwealth Avenue to the Chestnut Hill Reservoir. Because the city dragged its feet on this project, it was carried to completion only in the early 1890s. Since Commonwealth Avenue developed more slowly than Beacon Street it did not acquire a streetcar line until 1909. By the late 1890s, two major avenues ran along the periphery of the Aberdeen section, beckoning to potential commuters, with Beacon Street at first serving as the primary approach.

On August 9, 1890, the *Brighton Item* listed the advantages of Aberdeen to potential home builders in the following glowing terms:

Several feet above any considerable portion of land in the neighborhood, commanding magnificent views in every direction, well-watered, a perfect combination of woodland and glade, and admitting the free exercise of the artistic taste of the landscape gardener, these lands are sure to be sought for residential purposes by the most desirable buyers.

The neighborhood derives its name from the Aberdeen Land Company, which was founded in 1890. The company's stock was held by twenty-five investors, mostly Boston-area financiers, merchants and manufacturers. It was chartered to operate until 1915 for the express purpose of developing the area residentially. One of its largest stockholders was Henry M. Whitney, the transportation mogul who had developed Beacon Street. Others included G.T.W. Braman, president of the Boston Water Power Company; Noah W. Jordan, president and chairman of the board of the American Loan and Trust Company; and Isaac T. Burr, president of the Bank of North America. Two of the largest stockholders, incidentally, were Brighton men, George A. Wilson and Benjamin F. Ricker. As prior owners of land in the area, they probably traded their acreage for Aberdeen Land Company stock.

While there were other land companies that held property in the neighborhood—one being Henry Whitney's own West End Land Company—there seems little question that its present design—its street patterns and place names are a legacy of the Aberdeen Land Company.

The company was named for a Scottish county and many of the streets in Aberdeen likewise bear Anglo-Scottish names: Lanark, Sutherland, Kinross, Orkney, Strathmore, Radnor, Windsor and Warwick, among others.

How are we to account for this unusual nomenclature? The British Empire was at the height of its prestige in the 1890s; also, the works of the immensely popular novelist Sir Walter Scott had given a special aura of romanticism to things Scottish. These Anglo-Scottish shire names thus carried just the right hint of prestige and exclusiveness that Aberdeen's projectors wished to attach to their emergent elite neighborhood.

27

BRIGHTON'S ELITE
ABERDEEN NEIGHBORHOOD

L arge-scale residential development of Brighton's Aberdeen Section began with the introduction in 1889 of electric streetcar service along Beacon Street. Service to the Reservoir Station by train had been relatively inconvenient, cars running only once an hour. Electric streetcars, by contrast, began operating at 6:00 a.m. and ran at convenient ten-minute intervals during the busiest hours of the day.

The Aberdeen neighborhood experienced its first boom in house construction from 1889 to 1893, after which the building rate slowed for several years due to the depression of 1893. Rapid construction resumed, however, in the late nineties. By 1900 the Aberdeen district contained a total of 81 structures, all of them private residences. By 1910, 110 houses and 9 apartment buildings stood in Aberdeen. The early apartment structures were relatively small in scale (typically two- or three-story row house buildings). After 1915, however, many larger apartment buildings were constructed. By 1930 a majority of the district's housing units consisted of apartments.

The neighborhood's commercial center, Cleveland Circle, developed between 1910 and 1925. The square was named for former U.S. President Grover Cleveland shortly after his death in 1908.

What makes the Aberdeen Section unique is the successful integration of the built environment with the area's topography. In other neighborhoods, developers typically laid out a grid of streets before which all obstacles were obliged to give way. In Aberdeen, by contrast, curvilinear roadways wind their way through hilly, wooded and rocky terrain. Here topography and architecture achieved a remarkable integration. Imposing Shingle, Queen

Anne, Jacobean and Colonial Revival mansions lay perched atop giant pieces of ledge. The unique character of this Aberdeen neighborhood elicited the following amazed reaction from a *Boston Globe* writer who visited the district in 1892: "Over the Chestnut Hill Reservoir where the Aberdeen Land Company is building, there is one of the most unique sights I ever looked upon. Houses are rising from the solid rocks as if by magic, and it is worth one's while to make a long journey to see this grand transformation scene."

The structures built in Aberdeen between 1890 and 1930, whether single homes or apartment buildings, were of a uniformly high quality. The Sutherland Apartments, at 1714–1742 Commonwealth Avenue, is a case in point. This massive forty-bay structure near the Sutherland Road intersection, dating from 1914, designed by noted architect J.A. Halloren, is one of Boston's best examples of the Jacobean style.

Brighton's Aberdeen district attracted many distinguished residents, including two mayors of the city of Boston, a superintendent of the Boston public schools, an associate justice of the Massachusetts Supreme Judicial Court and a former congressman.

One of these mayors was the immensely popular and highly respected Patrick Collins, the city's second Irish mayor, who held office from 1902 until his untimely death in 1905. He had earlier served in the U.S. Congress and as American Consul General in London. Mayor Collins and his wife, Mary, lived at 74 Corey Road at the northern end of the district. Their residence was the first dwelling constructed on the Aberdeen section of Corey Road.

Some three decades later, in the late 1930s, another Boston mayor, Maurice Tobin, took up residence in Aberdeen. His wife, Helen, had grown up in the neighborhood. When her father, David Noonan, a stock broker, died in 1937, the newly elected mayor and his wife moved to 11 Kinross Road to be with Helen's widowed mother, though the Tobins remained there only briefly.

Boston Public Schools Superintendent Stratton D. Brooks lived at 97 Kilsyth Road for many years. One of the longest serving superintendents in the history of the Boston public schools, Brooks took charge of the system in 1906, presiding over it when it was at the height of its prestige.

Massachusetts Supreme Judicial Court Justice Henry King Braley, a former mayor of Fall River, moved to 151 Kilsyth Road in 1902, shortly after being appointed to the state's highest court. Another judge who resided in Aberdeen in the early years of the century was Josiah S. Dean, special justice of the South Boston Municipal Court, who lived at 19 Lanark Road. Prominent attorney Joseph F. O'Connell, who had served in the U.S. Congress from 1906 to 1910 while living in Dorchester, moved to 155 Kilsyth Road in the 1930s.

The quality of much of the residential development in Aberdeen is captured in this contemporary photograph of 131 Kilsyth Road, a handsome Shingle-style house designed by architect W.F. Goodrich. *Photo by William P. Marchione.*

Many prominent businessmen also established residences in Aberdeen in the early years of the century. Horace Phipps, president of Phipps Stained Glass Company, constructed a large house at 92 Chiswick Road. Phipps also built 109 Strathmore Road. The Phipps Mansion is gone, having been replaced by an apartment building. One wonders how much stained glass this manufacturer used in the construction of his Aberdeen residence.

Another interesting early resident was Andrew Morton, a wealthy manufacturer of steam and gas fixtures. The Mortons lived originally at 358 Chestnut Hill Avenue, in a house facing Cleveland Circle. About 1900, however, they moved to an elaborate new residence at 248 Chestnut Hill Avenue in the so-called New Aberdeen section, the area west of Commonwealth Avenue, which began experiencing large-scale development at a somewhat later date than the more easterly part of the neighborhood. Morton hired the great landscape architect Frederick Law Olmsted to lay out the grounds of his new residence. Sadly, in 1924 the mansion was taken down to clear the way for the Alexander Hamilton Elementary School, and its Olmsted-designed grounds were obliterated to make way for a schoolyard.

At 83 Sutherland Road once stood the elaborate mansion of William Howe Downes, author, historian and the highly respected art critic of the old *Boston Transcript*.

While Aberdeen's Phipps, Morton and Downes Mansions have disappeared, many equally imposing residences remain, testifying to the special character of this elite enclave.

At 77 Englewood Avenue stands a French château–style edifice built for Mr. and Mrs. Brackley Shaw in the early 1890s. Mr. Shaw was a prominent shoe manufacturer. The house, now a synagogue, was designed by C. Howard Walker, an architect with an international reputation, who later headed the Department of Design at the Museum of Fine Arts and also served as editor of the *Architectural Review*.

At 89 Englewood Avenue stands one of the oldest of the neighborhood's large-scale residences, an elaborate brick Queen Anne–style mansion, built in the late 1880s for roofing contractor Frank W. Krogman. The architect of the Krogman house was C.R. Beal.

Also impressive is a large stone and shingle manor house at 14 Selkirk Road. This lavishly detailed seventeen-room mansion, designed by G.D. Mitchell, and dating from 1899, sits high off the street on a piece of ledge. It was built for Charles A. Walker, a leading Boston painter, engraver and watercolorist who served for a time as vice-president of the Boston Art Club.

As befits a neighborhood of such stylistic vitality, a number of architects took up residence in Aberdeen. These included Edward Little Rogers, who designed a series of Aberdeen houses for his own use, prior to relocating in New York City. This most prolific of Aberdeen architects designed at least eighteen of the neighborhood's private residences. Other resident architects included William H. Andrews, who lived at 22 Sutherland Road and Edward H. Hoyt, who resided at 24 Cummings Road.

Especially worthy of note are three magnificent stone mansions at the northern end of the district, all built in 1910 for William H. Munroe, a Brighton businessman and landowner, on a speculative basis. One of these houses, 1642 Commonwealth Avenue (formerly the Hasiotis Funeral Home), is conspicuously sited and handsomely landscaped. The other Munroe houses, at 4 and 8 Egremont Road, though less conspicuous, are also quite impressive. The architect of all three stone structures was Harry M. Ramsey.

28

The Charles River Speedway
A Special Local Institution

In the late nineteenth and early twentieth centuries, the Metropolitan Parks Commission (predecessor of the Metropolitan District Commission) gradually transformed the unattractive marshes and mudflats that lined the Charles River between Watertown and downtown Boston into a magnificent eighteen-mile-long public park, considered by some to be Boston's greatest recreational facility. As has been noted by more than one commentator, this splendid centrally located swath of urban green space, known as the Charles River Reservation, performs the same function for densely populated Boston that Central Park does for the urban masses of New York City.

The most important step toward the development of the Charles River Reservation was the construction, from 1906 to 1910, of a dam near the mouth of the river (the Museum of Science sits atop the dam today), which permanently excluded the tides from the river, thereby permitting systematic improvement of the shoreline.

But years before the building of the dam, two major recreational facilities already existed at the river's edge, protected from tidal inundation by embankments or dykes. The first of these, the Charlesbank Park, the nation's first urban playground, was built adjacent to the city's West End in the late 1880s, chiefly as a place of resort for the residents of Boston's crowded downtown neighborhoods.

The second of these recreation grounds was built on the Allston-Brighton shore—the Charles River Speedway—and was the first major improvement of the westerly section of the reservation. It was built from 1898 to 1899, a full decade before the exclusion of the tides. Many long-term residents of Allston-Brighton have fond memories of attending racing events at the unique and historic Charles River Speedway, which existed into the 1960s.

The speedway complex included a mile-long publicly owned race course, used mostly for sulky racing, which extended from a point just east of the Arsenal Street Bridge to the great bend in the river, adjacent to Soldier's Field, passing over the sites now occupied by Artesani and Herter Parks. The complex also featured a 1.75-mile-long driveway, the original Soldier's Field Road, which paralleled the race course, but extended three quarters of a mile farther east, ending at the foot of Cambridge Street. The Charles River Speedway was also provided with a bicycle-racing course, that sport then being enormously popular.

The speedway was designed by the Olmsted landscaping firm (the founder, Frederick Law Olmsted, the renowned designer of New York's Central Park and Boston's Emerald Necklace park system, had by that date retired from the business, leaving his son and nephews in charge). Since the river was still subject to tidal flooding, the various components were built on a dam that stood some five feet above high water.

The Olmsted brothers also selected a fourteen-thousand-square-foot parcel of land at the western end of the speedway for the construction of an administration building, which included the speedway superintendent's office and residence, as well as accommodations for the police force and maintenance crew that patrolled and maintained the speedway. This rambling S-shaped shingle-clad building occupied a highly visible gateway location at the intersection of Western Avenue and Soldiers Field Road, and is the only portion of the speedway complex that still exists.

The designer of the Speedway Administration Building was the important architectural firm of Stickney and Austin. Frederick W. Stickney (1858–1918) studied architecture at MIT, graduating with honors in 1877. His principal works included Lowell's Memorial Hall and the Billerica Town Hall. His associate, William D. Austin (1856–1944), designed the Framingham Normal School, Charlestown High School and the original Administration Building at the East Boston Airport. Locally they also designed the Gardner Elementary School in North Allston. Austin served as president of the Boston Society of Architects for many years and authored a history of that organization.

The surviving Speedway Administration Building has considerable architectural and historical importance. The Boston Landmarks Commission's 1978 inventory of Allston-Brighton architecture described this rambling structure as the best example of Shingle-style architecture in the general area. A subsequent BLC inventory, dating from 1995, described

The Charles River Speedway

This 1902 photograph shows hundreds of sulkies gathered at the Charles River Speedway, Allston-Brighton's mile-long raceway on the banks of the Charles River, for the Third Annual Speedway Parade. *Courtesy of the Brighton-Allston Historical Society Archives.*

it as "an artful blend of the Shingle, Queen Anne, and Colonial Revival styles."

The Speedway Administration Building is important for two reasons: this handsome, architecturally distinguished structure, occupies a highly conspicuous location; it is also the last remnant of a recreational complex of national significance.

One of the key functions that the Charles River Speedway was intended to serve was to accommodate recreational vehicles that had previously used the Brighton Road (the portion of Commonwealth Avenue lying west of Kenmore Square) and neighboring Beacon Street in Brookline for racing and sleighing. As these roadways experienced increased development at the turn of the century, the Metropolitan Parks Commission sought to shift the locus of such activities to the edge of the Charles River in Allston-Brighton. This effort met with some initial resistance, however, as the following account from the book *The Driving Clubs of Greater Boston* suggests:

> *With the beginning of the 1904 sleighing season, the Selectmen of Brookline issued a notice forbidding racers to sleigh over the Beacon Street boulevard, which for years had been the sleighing ground for the horsemen of Boston. This so stirred up a lot of road drivers, who in the order thought they saw a movement to compel them to race over the Charles River Speedway, that a committee of them went to Henry M. Whitney, citizen of Brookline, and asked him to intercede for them with the Selectmen in having*

141

the ban removed. Mr. Whitney succeeded in doing so, but it proved later
that Beacon Street boulevard, as a popular resort in racing, was doomed.

The speedway was also significant as a bicycle course, one of only two in the United States designed by the Olmsted firm. Professor Robert McCullough of the University of Vermont Historic Preservation program, the author of *The Landscape of Community*, a specialist in transportation history, has described the Charles River Speedway and its bicycle-racing course as a nationally significant recreational facility.

Attesting to the great popularity of the Charles River Speedway in the early years of the twentieth century, was the 1903 construction, on an adjoining parcel of privately owned land, of an elaborate clubhouse and stables by the Gentlemen's Driving Club of Boston. It was here, on October 10, 1904, that the Metropolitan Driving Club of Boston was founded, an organization that counted among its members the aforementioned Henry M. Whitney, the transportation mogul and land speculator who had previously redesigned Brookline's Beacon Street into a Parisian-style grand boulevard. Club membership quickly mounted, and within weeks the fledgling organization had signed up 250 horsemen.

While the speedway, which had cost more than a million dollars to construct, was a publicly owned facility, it was the privately owned adjacent Metropolitan Driving Club that sponsored most of the racing activities there. Sadly, the original clubhouse, a handsome shingle building with adjoining stables, survived only until August 14, 1932, when a spectacular fire destroyed the complex while taking the lives of forty-four valuable racing and saddle horses.

29

Harvard on the Charles

For the first nearly three hundred years of its history, Harvard University was largely confined to the area around Harvard Yard near Harvard Square. As late as 1869, the college had an enrollment of barely eleven hundred students, and a faculty of a meager twenty-four. Harvard spread to the banks of the Charles River only at the turn of the twentieth century as its enrollment and educational mission expanded.

So successful was this late nineteenth- and early twentieth-century enlargement of the campus from a stylistic standpoint—the predominant architectural medium being the Neoclassical style—that today's casual observer probably assumes that the university buildings on the river's edge date from the eighteenth century.

The successful integration of the old and the new portions of Harvard's campus was a truly great achievement, testimony both to the vision and energetic leadership of two Harvard presidents, Charles W. Eliot and A. Lawrence Lowell, as well as the great talent of the architects the university commissioned to carry out this singular expansion program.

Prior to 1900, the Charles River shoreline east of Boylston Street (now John F. Kennedy Street)—a district then known as Riverside—was one of the least attractive areas on the margin of the river. Prior to 1908, when a dam was built near the mouth of the Charles permanently excluding the tides, the expanding and receding shoreline made the acreage unsuitable for anything other than commercial and industrial uses. Riverside accordingly developed into a district clogged with unattractive structures—an unpleasant and ugly assortment of wharves, coal yards, storehouses, even a power plant.

An 1873 engraving of the Brighton Meadows, the area of the Charles River that Henry Wadsworth Longfellow and his Brattle Street, Cambridge neighbors bought and donated to Harvard College in order to prevent its becoming the site of a huge slaughterhouse. *Courtesy of the Brighton-Allston Historical Society Archives.*

This was also true, to a lesser degree, of the Allston shoreline, where docks and a coal company stood adjacent to the North Harvard Street Bridge, the wooden span that crossed the river on the site of the present Larz Anderson Bridge.

The first proposal for the development of the Charles River shoreline by Harvard was advanced in 1894, by the landscape architect and conservationist Charles Eliot, son of Harvard President Charles W. Eliot. It was young Eliot's suggestion that Harvard develop the more than one hundred acres that it owned on the Allston-Brighton side of the river.

This land came to Harvard as a result of two late nineteenth-century gifts. One of the parcels, the Brighton Meadows, was donated to the college in the early 1870s by the poet Henry Wadsworth Longfellow and several of his Brattle Street, Cambridge neighbors. Learning that a group of Brighton butchers was proposing to build a giant slaughterhouse, or abattoir, at the Brighton Meadows location, which would spoil their view of the river, these concerned property owners purchased the acreage and presented it to Harvard. The second gift, to be known as Soldiers Field, was deeded to the university in the 1890s by the banker-philanthropist Henry Lee Higginson (founder of the Boston Symphony Orchestra) to commemorate six of his Harvard classmates who had been killed in the Civil War.

Thus the first major Harvard buildings constructed on the river's edge went up on the Allston shore from 1897 to 1903, and consisted of athletic facilities. These included Carey Cage, dating from 1897 (a structure taken down in the late 1990s), with adjacent playing fields and wooden spectator stands. Then, in 1900, the handsome Newell Boat House was constructed

Harvard University's Harvard Stadium, situated in North Allston. It was the world's first massive structure of reinforced concrete as well as the first large arena for American college athletics. The stadium was designed by the distinguished architectural firm of McKim, Mead and White. *Courtesy of the Brighton-Allston Historical Society Archives.*

just west of the North Harvard Street Bridge, designed by the Peabody and Stearns, a building notable for its use of slate as a façade.

The next major Harvard edifice, dating from 1903, was Allston's massive Harvard Stadium, designed by the leading architectural firm of McKim, Mead and White. This stadium, which seats more than fifty thousand spectators, was the world's first massive structure of reinforced concrete, as well as the nation's first large arena for college athletics.

The oldest extant Harvard structure on the Cambridge shore was the Weld Boat House, just east of the Larz Anderson Bridge, which dates from 1907. Rowing is Harvard's oldest organized athletic activity, going back to 1852. This handsome masonry structure replaced a modest wooden building that boating enthusiast George Walker Weld had built for Harvard in 1890.

Harvard's adoption about 1910 of a new policy requiring lower classmen to live in university housing provided the major impetus for the acquisition and development of the Riverside acreage. It was hoped that this house system, in which students and junior faculty would live together, would serve to enhance intellectual communication. A. Lawrence Lowell, president of Harvard from 1909 to 1933, carefully supervised every aspect of the large-scale construction project to which the new housing policy gave rise.

As the Cambridge Historical Commission noted of these early twentieth-century Neoclassical structures, their architecture reflected "a conscious effort by the administration to extend the atmosphere of the old Harvard Yard to a new South Yard and thus…symbolize the continuity of the Harvard 'Collegiate Way of Life.'"

The first of the four great houses to be built on the Cambridge shore, Winthrop House, comprises two edifices, Standish and Gore Halls, both built in 1913. The latter structure is notable for its garden façade, recalling Hampton Court in England. Winthrop House was designed by another notable architectural firm, Shepley, Rutan and Coolidge, successors to the great H.H. Richardson.

Next came McClintock Hall, dating from 1925 and enlarged in 1930, a structure that has since been absorbed into the modern Leverett House complex.

Then in 1929 and 1930, two additional houses were constructed on the river's edge, anchoring the eastern and western ends of this massive ensemble. First came Dunster House, at the eastern end, then Eliot House at Memorial Drive and Boylston Street, directly opposite the Weld Boat House. Both were designed by Shepley, Bulfinch and Abbott.

The Harvard School of Business Administration, founded in 1908, had built in the meantime a magnificent new complex on the Allston shore east of the Larz Anderson Bridge, on land that was still being used for farming up to the time of its construction. Dating from the 1925 to 1927 period, this grid of Georgian Revival–style buildings, with the George F. Baker Library as its focal element, faced Cambridge and the river. The Business School complex, like neighboring Harvard Stadium, was a work of McKim, Mead and White.

Prior to 1913 the only bridge spanning the Charles in the vicinity of Harvard had been the old wooden drawbridge. The North Harvard Street Bridge was replaced in 1913 by the Anderson Memorial Bridge, a handsome Neoclassical-style brick and concrete span designed to blend with the architecture of Harvard's new riverfront buildings. Larz Anderson, U.S. Ambassador to Belgium, and an 1888 Harvard graduate, furnished the money for the structure in memory of his father, Nicholas Longworth Anderson of the Harvard class of 1858. However, the bridge is popularly referred to as the Larz Anderson Bridge.

The other Harvard-area span, the Weeks footbridge, was built in 1926 while the business school was under construction with the object of linking the Cambridge and Allston portions of the campus. This bridge, also Neoclassical in design and arguably the most handsome in the vicinity of the university, was named for U.S. Secretary of War John W. Weeks, a former U.S. Senator and mayor of Newton. The money for its construction was donated by thirteen friends and business associates of Weeks. It too was designed by McKim, Mead and White.

Thus, between 1897 and 1931 Harvard University completely altered the appearance of both sides of the Charles River near Harvard Square, thereby transforming one of the least attractive stretches of the river into an area of singular beauty.

30

Brighton's Paul Revere Pottery
An Inspiring Experiment in Social Philanthropy

The finely crafted dishes, cups, bowls, vases and other items produced between 1908 and 1942 by Boston's Paul Revere Pottery command hefty prices in today's active antique market. Their appeal is greatly enhanced by the unique and inspiring history of the pottery.

The pottery's story begins with the establishment of a club called the Saturday Evening Girls, which operated out of the North End Branch of the Boston Public Library, then situated in the North Bennett Street Industrial School.

Living conditions in the immigrant North End at the turn of the century were appalling. The tenements into which the neighborhood's residents crowded were old and dilapidated, being mostly three- to five-story walkup apartments that lacked private baths or central heating. Three out of four of these housing units shared toilets. One in six shared water. The district's child mortality rate was the highest in Boston. The North End was by far the most congested district in the city.

It was with a view to enriching the lives of the young women of the neighborhood that the Saturday Evening Girls Club was established by North End branch librarian Edith Guerrier, a twenty-nine-year-old woman from New Bedford who had attended the MFA's Museum School. Guerrier's goal was to furnish constructive afterhours activities for the daughters of the district's mostly Jewish and Italian immigrant families.

In her memoirs, published posthumously in 1992 under the title *An Independent Woman*, Guerrier recalled the little speech she gave at the club's first meeting:

Someday you girls are going to enter the business world. You will need to know how to use the tool called mind, so that you can do your own thinking. You will need to know how to cooperate, and how to give and take with good-humored self-control. You will need to have a well-informed mind, and if you are to win positions with people you respect and admire, you will need to have a sense of the values of good literature, good music, and good recreation.

The club's meetings always began with a business session (in which its members learned the value of cooperation and planning), followed by a story hour (to encourage reading), along with such intellectual and artistic activities as singing, dancing, playwriting and dramatic performances.

The Saturday Evening Club soon attracted the attention and support of an important Boston philanthropist, Helen Osborne Storrow, then serving as chairperson of a committee of the Boston School Department, established to look into the social service work of the Boston Public Library. Her husband, investment banker and progressive reformer James Jackson Storrow Jr., sat on the Boston School Committee. Without the unremitting support and generous financial backing of Helen Storrow, it is unlikely that the pottery venture would ever have emerged.

A Paul Revere Pottery catalogue cover showing one of its workers decorating a large vase outside the pottery's Brighton headquarters at 80 Nottinghill Road. *Courtesy of the Brighton-Allston Historical Society Archives.*

Another key figure in the Paul Revere Pottery story was Edith Brown, Guerrier's close friend. The two young women had met at the Museum School, and soon after become housemates. It was while they were traveling in Europe in early 1908 (a trip paid for by the ever-generous Mrs. Storrow), that the two hit upon the idea of establishing a pottery to provide the Saturday Evening Girls with reliable, healthy and financially rewarding employment.

Upon returning to Boston, Guerrier and Brown began experimenting with pottery making in the basement of the house they owned in Brookline's Chestnut Hill section. In 1909 Mrs. Storrow threw her financial resources behind the venture by buying a tenement at 18 Hull Street in the North End to serve as the pottery's headquarters. This structure stood but a short distance from the Old North Church where Paul Revere had hung his historic signal lanterns—thus the choice of the name Paul Revere Pottery for the enterprise.

The Hull Street building was quickly renovated to meet the needs of the pottery. A shop and kiln room were installed at the basement level, pottery workrooms occupied the first floor and an assembly room was established above that. The building's top floors contained "model" apartments. One of these units accommodated Guerrier and Brown. While the former acted as the pottery's business manager (in addition to continuing to serve as North End branch librarian), the latter—an artist by temperament as well as training—served as the pottery's artistic director.

What makes the story of the Paul Revere Pottery especially interesting were the superior working conditions that prevailed there in a day when the daughters of immigrants often labored in sweatshops for pitifully low wages. The workrooms at the Paul Revere Pottery, in contrast to the dreary and unhealthy factories of the day, were well lit, well ventilated and always decorated with flowers. And while the pottery's workers went about the business of creating beautiful handcrafted items, the works of Dickens, Shakespeare and other great authors were read aloud to them for their intellectual edification.

Wages and benefits at the Paul Revere Pottery were also much better than those available in factories. The workday at the pottery never exceeded eight hours, as compared to the ten to twelve hours in other establishments. In addition, Paul Revere workers got a half-day off on Saturdays (a full six-day workweek then being almost universal) as well as a two-week paid vacation every year.

Job training at the Paul Revere Pottery was also enlightened. New girls learned by sitting beside and assisting more experienced workers, a method of training echoing the dying apprenticeship system that had dominated the handicrafts trades before the rise of the factory.

Since Paul Revere ware proved immensely popular, the pottery's relatively cramped North End facility was soon outgrown, and the two Ediths began searching for a more ample suburban setting for their enterprise.

They thought they had succeeded in early 1915, when they made a down payment on a parcel of land near the old Belmont Reservoir, but this money was soon returned to them when the people of that upscale community raised objections to having a "foreign" enterprise in their midst. This reaction reflected the powerful anti-immigrant bias that then existed in the United States, and that was particularly strong in the more affluent suburbs. "We heard ourselves," Guerrier wrote in her memoirs, "described as factory owners who intended to bring to a peaceful neighborhood foreign laborers who might scatter bombs in the streets or burn up the town and roast its inhabitants in their beds."

A short time later the Paul Revere Pottery acquired a piece of land in the Aberdeen section of Brighton atop Nottingham Hill (later renamed Nottinghill), the highest elevation in that community. Guerrier described the hill on which the pottery's new home was built as a "puddingstone mass," over which "the dust of centuries had drifted until the stone was covered with a carpet of forest grass, shaded by oaks and white birches." The new location was an "Elysian spot," she recollected, "a place of "lush grass[es] starred with innocence, cinquefoil, mouse ear, and violets; [in which] gray squirrels leaped from limb to limb of the tall oaks; and robins and bluebirds sang in the birch copse."

The Paul Revere Pottery's new headquarters at 80 Nottinghill Road was built between September 16 and November 29, 1915—in a period of just ten weeks. This English-style stucco cottage, which Guerrier and Brown themselves designed, sat on a three-acre lot that commanded a stunning view of the surrounding countryside, in sharp contrast to the pottery's previous home in the congested and noisy North End.

The first gathering of the workforce at the new site occurred on Thanksgiving Day in 1915. The pottery's employees then comprised twelve Jewish and Italian girls (who commuted to the site by streetcar from their homes in the central city), an English "jigger man" (a pottery wheel operator), two Italian potters and an Italian evangelical minister (Antonio Santino), whose job it was to fire the kiln and to act as watchman. Shortly thereafter Guerrier and Brown themselves took up permanent residence at Nottinghill.

The Paul Revere Pottery continued to operate from its Brighton headquarters until 1942, when its doors finally closed, ringing down the curtain on a unique and inspiring experiment in social improvement. The historic building still stands, having been converted into condominiums. It is a building of major importance in the history of social philanthropy.

31

BOSTON'S ORIGINAL AUTO MILE

No single technological innovation of the twentieth century has had a greater impact upon the character and the quality of American life, both positively and negatively, than the automobile.

The headquarters of the auto industry in Boston for over a half-century was the so-called Auto Mile, now largely forgotten—that portion of Commonwealth and Brighton Avenues between the Boston University Bridge and Allston's Union Square.

The founder of the Auto Mile was the fascinating Alvan Tufts Fuller (1878–1958), a native of Malden, Massachusetts, who was a major figure in both the business and political history of Massachusetts. A champion bicycle racer in his youth, Fuller's business career began with his establishment of a bicycle shop in his hometown in 1895, which he soon after moved to Columbia Road in Boston. Fuller became convinced, however, that the future of transport belonged to the motor vehicle, and took bold steps to ensure himself a central role in the rise of that industry. After traveling to Europe in 1900 to investigate the fast-growing auto industry there, the ambitious young entrepreneur persuaded the Packard Motor Company of Detroit, Michigan, to make him its exclusive dealer in the Boston area. A year later he added a Cadillac agency to his dealership, which was then located in the Motor Mart Building, in Boston's Park Square, a facility he shared with other Boston auto dealers.

In 1908 Fuller decided to move his growing dealership to an undeveloped tract at the intersection of Commonwealth and Brighton Avenues in Allston, a location known, by strange coincidence, as Packard's Corner, having been named for a well-known stable and riding school run by John D. Packard at 25 Brighton Avenue.

At this Packard's Corner location Fuller established the first combined auto salesroom and service station in New England. The massive facility comprised a sales salon and offices at the ground level, with the remainder of the building providing assembly, storage and repair facilities.

Fuller's handsomely furnished showroom had high ceilings and fluted columns and was lit by a combination of elaborate hanging fixtures and a barrel-vaulted skylight. Historian Chester Liebs tells us, "customers could bask in the prestige of a grand interior space, relax, and survey the cars exhibited around them."

The architect of Fuller's dealership was Albert Kahn, who was on his way to becoming the nation's leading specialist in automotive-related structures. Kahn had designed the Packard Motor Company's home office in Detroit. Other automotive structures by Kahn included the Ford Motor Company's Highland Park, Michigan plant, as well as Ford's enormous River Rouge complex in Dearborn, Michigan.

After establishing his Packard's Corner dealership on a solid footing, Fuller pursued one of the most interesting political careers in Massachusetts history—a career characterized by the same daring and brashness that so often marked his business ventures.

His rise in the political arena, like his rise in business, was amazingly rapid—catapulting Fuller from a seat in the state legislature into the Massachusetts governorship in a single decade. Always a political adventurer, Fuller entered electoral politics in 1914 under the banner of Teddy Roosevelt's Progressive Party, winning a seat in the Massachusetts House of Representatives by the razor-thin margin of just sixteen votes.

Then, in 1916 Fuller successfully challenged a nine-term congressman for a seat in the U.S. House of Representatives, once again winning by the narrowest of margins. In 1920, in another long-shot candidacy, he took on the powerful speaker of the Massachusetts House of Representatives in a quest for the lieutenant governorship, winning both the primary and general election. Finally, in 1924 Alvan Fuller capped his amazing political career by capturing the governorship, defeating Democratic gubernatorial candidate James Michael Curley in the process.

While the popular Fuller easily won reelection to the governorship in 1926, his political career ended abruptly when he relinquished that office in 1929 at the age of only fifty-one. Fuller's political demise was occasioned by two factors—a decline in the fortunes of the Republican Party in the Depression era, and Fuller's 1927 refusal to commute the death sentences of the immigrant radicals Sacco and Vanzetti who had been sentenced to death in a trial filled with irregularities. Had Fuller's controversial Sacco-Vanzetti decision not sullied his reputation with Americans of immigrant stock, one commentator suggests he might well have received the 1932 Republican vice-presidential nomination.

But it is Fuller's contributions to the Auto Mile that chiefly concern us, and there can be little question of his success in that regard.

Other dealers were quick to follow Fuller to the Packard's Corner area in the century's second decade. In 1912 Kissel Kars built a nearby showroom, and in 1913 the White Motor Company followed suit. By 1919 there were at least a dozen dealerships lining Commonwealth and Brighton Avenues and Boston's Auto Mile had been solidly established.

Alvan Tufts Fuller's vast auto dealership at Packard's Corner, Allston. The building still stands, having been converted to condominiums in the 1980s. *Courtesy of the Brighton-Allston Historical Society Archives.*

An interior view of another Allston auto dealership, Commonwealth Chevrolet, later known as Oste Chevrolet. This building now houses a Shaw's supermarket. *Courtesy of the Brighton-Allston Historical Society Archives.*

The Auto Mile experienced its fastest period of expansion in the 1920s. On the eve of the Depression, no fewer than 117 automobile-related business establishments lined Commonwealth and Brighton Avenues. While the number shrank by about one-third during the Depression, the district survived.

Even at the depths of the economic turndown, in 1932 the Auto Mile was home to no fewer than fifty-four car dealerships specializing in a combination of new, used and commercial vehicles, dealerships selling all of the following makes, many of which no longer exist: the Auburn, Cord, Oldsmobile, Ford, Hupmobile, Cadillac, Franklin, LaSalle, Pontiac, Chevrolet, Chrysler, Plymouth, Reo, Nash, Buick, Packard, Pierce-Arrow, Rolls-Royce, Studebaker and Stutz.

The heart of the Auto Mile remained Packard's Corner. In the immediate vicinity were concentrated ten dealerships, some of the largest in the district, including Auburn Motor Cars (an Auburn and Cord dealership), Boston Hupmobile, Clark-Crowley Motors (a Pontiac dealership), the Packard Motor Car Company (Fuller's pioneer Packard and Cadillac dealership), Pierce-Arrow Cars and Rolls-Royce of America.

Truck dealerships also located in the general area, tending to cluster at the western end of the district. By 1932 some seven truck dealerships had taken up residence on North Beacon Street, west of Union Square, including the Mack Motor Truck Company at number 95 and the General Motors Truck Company at 103 North Beacon Street. Number 61 North Beacon Street housed another important truck dealership, the International Harvester Company of America.

While a serious contraction of the auto sales industry occurred during the Second World War, owing to wartime shortages, with the war's end the industry quickly rebounded, attaining its highest level of prosperity between 1950 and 1965.

The most memorable of the many innovations that Alvan Fuller initiated were the open houses that his Packard Motor Company hosted annually on Washington's birthday, giving customers an opportunity to view the latest models and to plan future car purchases. By the 1920s other dealers were following Fuller's lead and Washington's birthday open houses became an event looked forward to with great anticipation by the general public.

The Auto Mile went into rapid decline in the late 1970s as many dealers moved their establishments to more accessible suburban locations. While there were still twenty-one dealerships in the general area as late as 1975, by 1981 only eleven remained. The Packard Motor Company building has been converted to condominiums. The neighboring Commonwealth Chevrolet Building has become a Shaw's Market. While a handful of auto dealerships still inhabit the Commonwealth and Brighton Avenue strip, they are but a pale reflection of the large-scale auto sales industry that once lined Boston's thriving Auto Mile.

32

BARRY'S CORNER
The Life and Death of a Neighborhood

The former residents of Barry's Corner, a tiny neighborhood that once stood at the northeast corner of Western Avenue and North Harvard Street in North Allston, will gather for their fifth biennial reunion on September 10, 1988.

Though Barry's Corner was demolished more than twenty years ago, it continues to inspire intense loyalty. What accounts for the powerful attachment this neighborhood continues to exert over its now widely dispersed population? Part of the explanation lies in the kind of place Barry's Corner was—a tightly knit neighborhood of strong personal relationships. Neighborhoods of that sort are fast disappearing from our society, so it is understandable that Barry's Corner is remembered by its former residents with great affection. But this unusually strong attachment has another, more powerful source. Reinforcing affection, lending it special intensity, is a shared memory of the heroic but ultimately unsuccessful struggle for survival that Barry's Corner waged against the powerful Boston Redevelopment Authority (BRA) and the indifference of the rest of Allston-Brighton.

A compact working-class neighborhood of 9.3 acres, Barry's Corner contained only fifty-two structures housing a total of just seventy-one families. Its ethnic composition was mostly Irish and Italian, with a sprinkling of Polish and French families.

Former resident Francis Bakke, who now lives in Framingham, describes Barry's Corner as "a good place to live. There was a lot of pride in our neighborhood. Children who grew up there often stayed on as adults. It was common to find three generations of a family living there." According to another former resident, Bernard Redgate, also of Framingham, what made life in Barry's Corner special was "a connection with people that you don't have in the suburbs."

Because the neighborhood was well served by public transportation (bus lines connected it to Union, Central and Harvard Squares), a family could get along without a car. Other amenities included a public park across North Harvard Street (Smith Playground) and proximity to St. Anthony's Church as well as public and parochial schools.

The first indication the neighborhood received of the city's demolition plans came in the spring of 1961. "It came like a bolt," noted Bakke. "We learned about it one night on the Channel 4 news. The city made no effort to notify us before that announcement."

The BRA's plan called for the demolition of the existing fifty-two structures and the construction on the cleared acreage (by well-connected developers) of a $4.5 million, ten-story, 372-unit luxury apartment building, to be paid for largely with federal money. The BRA contended that the Barry's Corner structures were blighted, a charge the residents hotly disputed. The authority likewise contended that the existing neighborhood was yielding the city relatively little tax revenue. The proposed luxury complex would pay $150,000 as compared

Left: The people of Barry's Corner waged a long, vigorous and heartfelt battle to save their neighborhood, as evidenced by signs such as this one that were displayed on their homes during the protracted struggle. *Courtesy of the Brighton-Allston Historical Society Archives.*

Opposite: In the end, the Boston Redevelopment Authority prevailed and Barry's Corner was obliterated. *Courtesy of the Brighton-Allston Historical Society Archives.*

to the paltry $15,000 the Barry's Corner properties were contributing. The BRA assured the public that "every effort is being made to assure that the residents now living in the area are provided with suitable new homes."

Barry's Corner residents were understandably outraged. The BRA was proposing to obliterate an entire neighborhood, to seize and demolish private homes so that luxury housing could be constructed and to pay for this questionable project with public money.

When the BRA finally came to the neighborhood for a public hearing on the proposal in June of 1962, a full year after the initial announcement, it was met by a firestorm of protest. "Members of the BRA," the press commented, "were visibly shaken by the hostile treatment they received."

Neighborhood spokesmen took the position that if public money was to be used in the area at all, it should be used to repair the existing streets and residential structures, rather than to increase Boston's supply of luxury housing. "We saw it as a clear case of robbing from the poor and giving to the rich," Francis Bakke asserted indignantly.

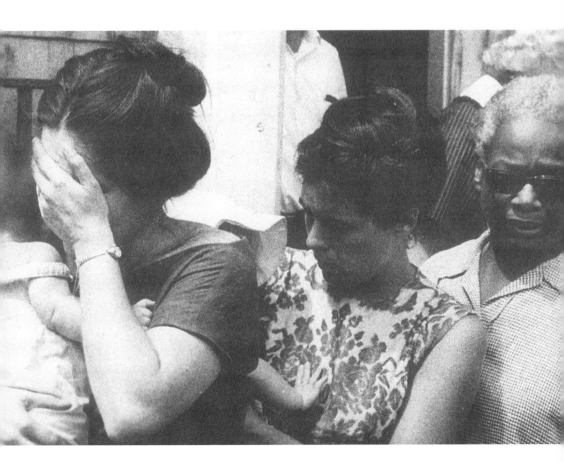

Father Timothy Gleason, pastor of St. Anthony's Church, observed at the June 1962 hearing that the City of Boston had neglected the area: "We've never even been given a finished street. Barry's Corner is not a slum area. These people are good, God-loving people. The word blighted means rot and decay. There is nothing rotten, nothing decayed in Barry's Corner." A large sign appeared soon after on the conspicuously situated front lawn of the Foricelli house on North Harvard Street containing the simple message, "To Hell With Urban Renewal!"

Residents left no stone unturned in their long and vigorous campaign to save the neighborhood. They appealed to every level of government for relief: Boston Mayor John F. Collins, the Boston City Council, the State Planning Board, the State Legislature, the Federal Department of Housing, mostly to no avail. They also organized the Citizens for Private Property, which issued a stream of impassioned press releases.

In December 1962, at a Boston City Council hearing, Barry's Corner residents "stoutly reaffirmed their pledge to hold onto their homes until they are driven out by force."

Barry's Corner suffered a major defeat in January 1963, however, when the Boston City Council approved the BRA's plan by a 5 to 4 vote. Outraged Barry's Corner residents responded by picketing Mayor John Collins's home in Jamaica Plain.

The first physical confrontation between residents and the city came in August 1964 when a BRA appraisal team was driven from the neighborhood. The local paper reported this event under the headline "Allston Minutemen Rout BRA":

> A horn blasted throughout the North Harvard Street area Tuesday noon, and some 30 citizens turned out in true minute-man fashion to rout an appraisal team from the Boston Redevelopment Authority.
>
> Homeowners mustered at Redgate's Store at 162 North Harvard Street armed with brooms, shovels, sticks and spades minutes after George Tetrault and Bernard Redgate drove through the neighborhood sounding the alert.

The four-year crusade to save the neighborhood had an effect. Public opinion seemed to be rallying to the cause. By early 1965 the Barry's Corner controversy was causing the Collins administration deep embarrassment.

Then, on July 22, 1965, the Massachusetts State Legislature passed a resolution opposing the Barry's Corner project. The neighbors also met the BRA's August 1965 evictions and demolition with "riotous protests," which generated more negative publicity for the BRA.

Two significant events quickly followed: demolition was suspended (however, forty of the fifty-two buildings at Barry's Corner had already come down at that point). The mayor also announced that the city was withdrawing the luxury apartment proposal. Instead, a blue ribbon panel would be established to reevaluate the situation. (This panel, in fact, recommended that the mayor turn back the deeds of the remaining homeowners if they would agree to rehabilitate their properties in accordance with BRA standards, but Mayor Collins and the BRA chose to ignore that advice.)

Instead, the contract to develop Barry's Corner was awarded to a local development team, the Committee for North Harvard (CNH), which was cosponsored by a number of local churches. The building that presently occupies the Barry's Corner site was built by CNH in 1969–70.

The remaining homeowners were deeply bitter over CNH's failure to make the return of their titles a part of its development plan. The leading spokesman of the neighborhood at this stage was Marjorie Redgate (mother of Bernard). The Redgates owned the only store in Barry's Corner, which had long served as a focal point of community activity. Mrs. Redgate, who later wrote a bitter four-hundred-page account of the Barry's Corner struggle entitled—like the famous sign—"To Hell With Urban Renewal!" Her account of the struggle to save Barry's Corner expressed deep disappointment at the failure of the Allston-Brighton community to lend its support: "People who say they are interested in us let these homes get pushed down by bulldozers. They didn't care about our titles. They forgot the rights of the individuals who lived there."

The Redgates and two other residents, Mary Casey and Eunice Hollum, held out to the bitter end, which came finally in October 1969.

The holdouts were joined by almost a hundred protestors, who, the press reported,

> *paraded up and down North Harvard Street in front of the homes chanting anti-urban renewal slogans and stating their determination to stay and support the three holdout families.*
>
> *It took a squadron of more than 50 Boston policemen to clear the area. In a flurry of shoving and fist-fighting the police dispersed the protesters and some members of the press, established police lines, and carted off a number of protesters to District 14 Police headquarters for booking on charges of illegal assembly.*

The last holdout was a weeping Marjorie Redgate. "I don't want you or the police to be hurt," she told the crowd. "We're all finished here."

Visit us at
www.historypress.net